LEM BANKER'S BOOK
OF SPORTS BETTING

SPORTS
BETTING

OTHER BOOKS BY FREDERICK C. KLEIN:

The Education of a Horse Player (with Sam Lewin)

News and the Market (with John Prestbo)

Bulls, Bears and Other Sports (editor)

LEM BANKER'S BOOK OF SPORTS BETTING

SPORTS BETTING

Lem Banker and Frederick C. Klein

E. P. DUTTON ■ NEW YORK

PUBLISHER'S NOTE: *The legality of sports betting and bookmaking is determined and regulated on a state-by-state basis by the individual states.*

*Published in the United States by
E. P. Dutton, a division of New American Library,
2 Park Avenue, New York, N.Y. 10016.*

Library of Congress Cataloging-in-Publication Data
Banker, Lem.
Lem Banker's book of sports betting.
1. Sports betting—United States. I. Klein, Fred (Frederick C.) II. Title.
GV717.B36   1986   796'.0973   86-8850
ISBN 0-525-48268-7

*Published simultaneously in Canada
by Fitzhenry & Whiteside Limited, Toronto.*

Designed by Nancy Etheredge

1   3   5   7   9   10   8   6   4   2

First Edition

To my father, Benjamin,
who told me that the harder I'd work,
the luckier I'd get.

L. B.

To my wife, Susie

F. K.

ACKNOWLEDGMENTS

Thanks to Mort Olshan of *The Gold Sheet* for the generous help he gave us in putting together this book, and for his unfailing thoughtfulness and integrity over the 30 years in which I've known him. Thanks to Howard Schwartz and Gentleman John Luckman of the Gamblers' Book Store and publishing company in Las Vegas for putting their keen minds and thousands of volumes at our disposal when we needed research assistance.

Larry Merchant, the author and sports commentator, came to Las Vegas in 1972 for my help in doing his wonderful book *The National Football Lottery*. We made believers of each other, and he encouraged me to begin the newspaper handicapping columns I enjoyed doing in the early 1970s. Later, David Israel helped me write another series of columns for the *Chicago Tribune*. Thanks to

Royce Feour, top sportswriter for the *Las Vegas Review-Journal,* who conscientiously edited my local column.

Thanks to Moe Goldberg, a lifelong friend, for always blaming my losers on the teams and attributing my winners to my skill and judgment.

Thanks to Bob Martin, odds maker, whose integrity and honesty helped make sports betting a recognized, legitimate business for the state of Nevada.

Thanks to Debbie, my loyal, beautiful, loving wife, for knowing that the rainbow was within reach for someone trying to make it as a professional gambler, against all odds.

L. B.

CONTENTS

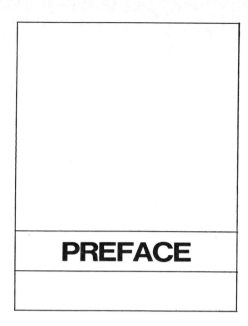

PREFACE

The low-slung Spanish-style house, set on a quiet street out of sight of the glitzy hotels of the Las Vegas "Strip," is fronted by rosebushes and a lush, green lawn tended by hired groundskeepers. Parked in the driveway is a white Mercedes-Benz convertible with a Nevada license plate that reads, simply, LEM. In the garage is a bronze Cadillac, the householder's family car.

At the rear of the place, in a walled backyard, is a tiled swimming pool, flanked by statuary and more rosebushes. Off to one side is a huge, signal-receiving dish that rotates on command of a console inside the house, to pick up television stations from across the country. Off to the other side is an outdoor gym complete with punching bag, inversion device, and weight rack. They're just the things for the sort of weight-trimming workouts that the fitness-conscious go in for these days.

The house itself isn't unusual for Las Vegas; plenty of rich people live there. Even so, its occupant stands out. He is a gambler, not a headline entertainer or casino operator, and a well-off gambler in this city of losers and hustlers is a rare bird.

"Plenty of guys try to make it as players out here, but very, very few succeed," says Lem Banker, the tall, trim, tanned lord of this particular manor. "They don't fail because they're stupid, but because the game and the 'vig' wear them down. By 'vig' I mean the vigorish. That's the house's cut—the eleven to ten odds that you bet into in most games, day in and day out. It's like a poker game where the houses reaches in and takes four-point-five percent of every pot. It's not much, but it adds up. If you play long enough, almost everybody at the table will wind up broke."

Lem Banker, however, has been a professional sports bettor for 34 of his 57 years, and the long run has yet to wear him down. In fact, the longer he plays, the more distance he puts between himself and penury. While he says that his precise annual income is a matter between himself, his accountant, and the Internal Revenue Service, he allows that it runs well into six figures.

Lem notes that he hasn't always lived in luxury. He has been broke and in debt, and needed to cash a $600 basketball bet to pay the medical expenses attending the birth of his daughter, Blaine, 25 years ago. ("Otherwise, the hospital might have kept her," he jokes.)

"But the difference between me and a lot of other guys is that I learned while I was losing," he says in the astringent tones of his native New Jersey. "I learned how to budget my time and how to handle my money. I learned to shop the odds. I learned not to overbet. I stick to the games I know—football, basketball, baseball, and boxing—and leave the rest alone. No cards, no horses, no tables: that's my motto. You have to know the limits of your knowledge.

"People ask me how they can do what I do. I tell 'em to work at it seventy hours a week, like me. The average guy, who has a regular job and likes to bet a few dollars on a game for fun, shouldn't expect the same results as a pro. He wouldn't expect to play golf just on Sundays and beat Jack Nicklaus, would he? But if he goes about it right, he can come out ahead and have a lot of fun. You can't ask more from a hobby than that."

For Banker, of course, gambling is a job, not a hobby. His "office hours" begin when he arises at about 10:00 A.M., which is early in the city with no clocks. They end only when he turns out the lights at around 2:00 A.M.

First on his agenda this day is a swim in his pool—he keeps the water cool because it wakes him up—followed by a breakfast of hot cereal, cornbread, a sweet roll, juice, and coffee. The swim will be the first of two workouts he'll take during the day, and the meal will be his last before dinner, which he eats at about eight o'clock in the evening. He is vain about his appearance, and believes that his diet, abstention from liquor, and vigorous physical regimen keep him mentally sharp for his chosen tasks. "Hot dogs, booze, and broads ruin more gamblers than sore-armed quarterbacks," he declares.

He then sits down with his newspapers to review the results of his previous day's wagers and post them in his account books in neat columns. The amounts he bets—and the number of games he plays—are large even by Las Vegas standards. During the football season, he'll typically risk between $3,000 and $20,000 a game on 12 to 15 college games and 6 to 10 professional contests every weekend. He'll bet lesser but still substantial amounts on as many as 100 college basketball games a week in season, and on 40 to 60 big-league baseball games a week.

He doesn't win all the time—nobody does—and he doesn't expect to. "I'm like a supermarket: I do a lot of volume, and hope to make a little profit," he says, smiling.

"Offer me 60 percent winners for the rest of my life and I'll take it right now and say 'Thank you. Thank you, very much.'"

He has pored over his numbers—the basis of his handicapping system—the night before, and at around noon he begins the shopping process that determines which bets he will make. He phones the dozen or so sports books around Las Vegas that offer telephone service for their prices on the seasonal games—on this day baseball—and carefully jots down the figures. One book, for example, may offer $1.30 for a $1.00 bet on the Atlanta Braves over the Philadelphia Phillies, and another may offer a return of $1.40 for the same wager. Using a computerized telephone hookup that dials his regular calls with a push of a code of just two numbers, he'll repeat this bargain-hunting routine several times during the day before placing his bets. "What you save is what you earn," says he.

Banker canvasses the betting parlors that don't transact business by phone with a team of runners who call him with prices and, at times, lay his wagers. The pay for this task is the chance to follow the master's bets. It's a job he has little trouble filling.

At around 1:00 P.M., Banker pries his ear off his telephone. Dressed in slacks, open-necked sportshirt, and thick, gold neck chain, he hops into his Mercedes and makes his rounds in the flesh. He sees and is seen, swaps wisecracks with his fellow plungers around the betting rooms, and, at times, makes man-to-man wagers with other gamblers, avoiding altogether the vig that the bookmaking shops charge.

Banker's procession along the Strip is attended by waves and greetings from well-wishers; he is a celebrity hereabouts because of his well-known acumen and his football-season newspaper betting columns in cities as far apart as New York and San Francisco. It is a point of pride with him that he has never accepted a paycheck for a "square" job. He turns over to charity his earnings from his columns and his frequent appearances on radio and television sports shows. He says he is collaborating on this book on his handicapping methods "to give the average guy a break" against the bookmakers. "Why should the bookies have all the fun?" he asks.

"You're Lem Banker, aren't you?" says a short, bespectacled tourist with a short, bespectacled woman, apparently his wife, in tow in the bright sunshine outside Caesars Palace Hotel on the Strip. Lem acknowledges his identity.

"Wow! This makes my day!" the man says, shaking Lem's hand. "By the way, who do you like in the Texas Rangers' game?"

"The White Sox," Lem answers.

"Me, too! Me, too!" says the fellow, alight.

"Nice guy," says Lem with a shrug when the man is out of earshot. "Usually, they ask who I like first, and say hello later."

Information is gambling's lifeblood, and inside the hotel's towering sports book Lem gets one of his several transfusions of the day. This is the week of the Marvin Hagler–Thomas Hearns world's middleweight championship prizefight in Las Vegas, and the Strip is abuzz with gossip about the match. Having studied the odds (favoring Hearns) and the fighters, Lem has picked Hagler. He started with a "small" bet of $5,000, but is considering raising it. Now a stocky, red-haired man sidles up to him and whispers good tidings.

"I hear that Hearns is having trouble with his legs in training. Pulled a muscle a week or so ago," the man confides.

Lem has some information of his own to impart. "A doctor I know at a hospital downtown says his partner saw Hearns for a mouth cut a couple of days ago," he tells the man. "Says he would have put a couple of stitches in it, but with the fight so close, he didn't. He says it's no big deal, but it could give Hearns trouble."

Both men nod sagely. When the other departs, Lem decides to raise his wager on Hagler. "Half the stuff like that you hear is bull, but it's all going the same way—against Hearns," he says. "Besides, the more I think of it, the more I like Hagler. The guy is fighting at his natural weight while Hearns is moving up, and Hagler *looks* like a fighter. It's the pit bull versus the poodle."

Lem eventually persuades himself to put $25,000 on Hagler's shaven pate in the match, mostly at favorable odds. On the day of the fight the odds shift sharply toward Hagler. For a change, the "smart money" is right. Hagler scores a technical knockout over the slender, curly haired Hearns in the third round. Lem watches it from a $600 ringside seat. Among his guests is actor Lee Majors, a friend.

Lem figures he has the win coming, having lost his previous three prizefight bets, all on underdogs. After the fight, Hearns says he was bothered by "tightness" in his legs. He doesn't mention the cut mouth.

From Caesars, Lem proceeds to the Churchill Downs Sports Book, a storefront operation about two furlongs down the Strip. While Lem banters with the regulars watching baseball on television out front, the book's long-time manager, Frank Hall, tells a visitor why Lem has made it where others come up short. "Lem doesn't try to make yesterday's bets good, and he's got control—he doesn't chase bad money," says Hall, peering over his half-glasses. "Too many customers like him, we close our doors."

Back home after a couple more stops, Lem is greeted outside his front door by Pete, one of seven cats kept by him and his wife, Debbie, along with Melba, an old German shepherd. Pete, a muscular, all-black cat, is clearly Lem's favorite. "Look at this animal! He's the Sonny Liston of cats!" Lem enthuses. "Not only is he unbeaten in fights, but he's the father of every kitten in the neighborhood."

That launches Lem into a story about how he came to be a cat owner. "I think it was 1966—the Chicago Bears and the Green Bay Packers were playing a preseason game," he says. "The Packers had a great team that year, and they were favored, but they had nothing to prove in the game, so I liked the Bears. The game opens with the Packers a six-point favorite. It goes to six-and-a-half, seven and seven-and-a-half. I'm taking the Bears all the way. I get three or four thousand dollars down on the game. That was big money for me then.

"I'm at home in our apartment, all nervous, waiting for the game to start, when my daughter comes in with a stray cat. She wants to know if she can keep it. I tell her to be quiet while the game is on. The Bears win, and I win my bet. I'm happy, so I tell her she can keep it. The money I won was part of the downpayment on this house. Since then, we've always thought that cats were lucky."

Now it is time for an hour in the sun to freshen his tan. Lem dons brief black swimming trunks and stretches out on a chaise longue by his pool. He's not there five minutes when the phone starts to ring. His runners phone in odds-line changes; cronies call to ask who he likes in the evening's baseball games and in the fight. He reveals his choices to one and all. "My bets are down," he explains. "Why shouldn't I tell my friends what I'm doing?"

He puts in a brisk half-hour with his weights and heavy punching bag, working up a good sweat. He was a regular jogger and bicycle rider until he fell off his bike after hitting a bump and injured his hip and leg a few months before. The parts were mending nicely and he expected to be back on the track within weeks (he was).

Then he uses his home steambath for a half-hour, showers, dresses, and sits down in front of one of the dozen or so television sets in his home to take in a baseball game. He watches with the sound low, reading letters from a stack of mail and various newspaper sports pages he has accumulated. In the background, a Sportsticker clicks out a paper tape of inning-by-inning scores of other baseball games around the country. Lem pays $340 a month for the year-round service. He says it's worth the money "to keep on top of things." He explains that complete attention to the game at hand isn't necessary. He watches games mainly to get a "feel" for the teams and their players. Like his approach to football and basketball, his betting on baseball revolves mainly around the figures he gleans from the teams' past performances (more about this later). "You're better off watching games with one eye, just to follow the flow of the action," he says. "You only watch most teams once in a while, and if you take what you see too seriously, your idea of a team can get distorted by one especially good or bad game."

Dinner this night consists of roast chicken at home with Debbie, the slim former fashion model he met back home in New Jersey, but often as not they'll dine out. Usually he'll take a nighttime tour of his stops along the Strip before settling down at his kitchen table at about 11:00 P.M., away from the jangling telephones of the day, for about two hours of concentrated study of the next day's or weekend's games. He can't understand how other gamblers can do their "homework" amid the hubbub of the betting parlors.

"When I'm home, by myself, the numbers talk to me," he says. "It's just me and them with nobody else in the way. Since I started really paying attention to them, I've never gone very far wrong."

FREDERICK C. KLEIN

LEM BANKER'S BOOK OF SPORTS BETTING

SPORTS BETTING

SPORTSMAN'S PRAYER

Dear Lord, in the battle that goes on through Life
I ask but a field that is fair,
A chance that is equal with all in the Strife,
A Courage to strive and to dare.
And if I should win, let it be by the Code
With my Faith and Honor held high.
And if I should lose let me stand by the road
And cheer as the Winners go by.

—FROM LEM BANKER'S UNION CITY, NEW JERSEY,
HIGH SCHOOL YEARBOOK

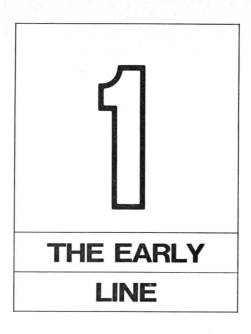

THE EARLY
LINE

My real name is Lester, but only my wife calls me that. Everybody else calls me Lem. I picked that name myself when I was a kid, because I thought that Lester, or Les, sounded sissy. When I think of some of the things I've been called since, Lester doesn't sound too bad at all.

My family name originally wasn't Banker. We picked that up when my grandfather came to the United States from Russia. My forebears on both sides lived in Russia. I don't know what they did there, but if you saw the movie *Fiddler on the Roof* you probably have a pretty good idea. We Jews didn't own many banks in that country.

I was born on May 4, 1927, in the Bronx, New York. My father's name was Benjamin, and my mother's was Edith. My dad fought in World War I. I have an older sister named Joyce. Two kids was a small family in those days. My father had 11 brothers and sisters, and my mom had 12, or maybe it was the other way around.

At one time, when I was little, my family was pretty well off financially. My dad and a few of his brothers owned a company in New York City that made combs and brushes out of celluloid, which was the forerunner of plastic. They bought their raw materials from the Du Pont Company. Then Du Pont decided to manufacture the same items, and my dad's company went out of business.

About that same time the Depression hit. Jobs were scarce, so Dad opened a little confectionery store on Bergenline Avenue in Union City, New Jersey. He sold candy and ice cream, cigars and newspapers. Dad was always a good hustler who tried to put away an extra dollar or two for the family, so right away he put a punchboard in the place. People would pay a nickel or a dime for a number that might win them a prize. Pretty soon he was taking small bets on the horses and the baseball games. It wasn't long before the bookmaking part of his business got to be the main thing, and selling candy became the sideline.

You think of a bookmaking joint today and you picture big-time gangsters, but it wasn't that way then. Betting was casual, out in the open, and a way of life with a lot of people. Of course, my dad turned over half the money he took in to the "boys" who ran the gambling in our town, and they paid off the cops. But that was no secret, either. People would come right in the front door of Dad's place and bet. Customers were neighborhood people who'd place $2.00 or $5.00 on a horse or ballgame once in a while. In the 1930s, a $10 bet was a big deal, although once World War II started, and the people got good-paying jobs in the defense plants, the action picked up quite a bit.

I got my love of sports from my dad, who was a great fan. He didn't go in much for exercise himself—people in those days thought that resting was better for you than working out—but he was a good pool player and he loved watching baseball and boxing. We'd go to the Bronx to watch the Yankees play. Lou Gehrig was my favorite ball player. We'd also go to the fights. I saw all the great fighters of the 1930s and 1940s: Joe Louis, Tony Galento, Max Baer, Jersey Joe Walcott, Beau Jack, Rocky Graziano, and all those guys. We'd go to the local fight clubs, too. I remember going to school sleepy a lot of days because my dad had taken me to a fight the night before.

I was always tall—I get my height from my mother's side—and I liked to play sports more than watch them. Basketball was my favorite, but I played all the others, too. My folks never had a hard time finding me when I was a kid. I was always at the playground, playing one game or another.

By the time I enrolled in Union Hill High School in Union City, I was almost six feet tall, and I was six-foot-three when I graduated, the same height I am now. I played center on the basketball team, end on the football team, and I threw the shotput in track.

Basketball was my best sport. I had a terrific left-handed hook shot. In one game against Weehawken High I scored 28 points, which was just 4 points short of the county record. I would have broken the record if I hadn't gotten in a fight with the other center, which got us both thrown out of the game. He started it. I think he did it because he didn't want me to break the record against him. You've got to remember that 28 points was an awful lot in those days. Forty-five points for a whole team was a big score then.

In my senior year, 1945, Union Hill made it to the finals of the New Jersey state high school basketball tournament, but we lost there to Camden High. I made all-state and got some scholarship offers. I took the summer off to work in the Catskill Mountains, in New York, and think them over.

I'd worked at the President's Hotel in the Catskills a couple of summers before that, lifeguarding and playing basketball. Basketball was a big thing there at the time. All the resorts had teams, and they'd play each other at night. High school players like me would get $5 or $10 a game; the college players would get more. I played against some of the best players in America in the Catskills. Bob Cousy was with Tamarack Lodge, and "Easy Ed" Macauley, the six-foot-eight guy who played for St. Louis University and the Boston Celtics, was up there, too. I have to say that I could hold my own in any company.

That summer stands out in my mind because of an argument I got into with my dad about gambling. I always was good with numbers, and I'd help him tally the betting slips in his shop in the evenings. But I'd never done any betting myself or gotten involved in his business in any other way. One day, though, I was at the pool at the President's, and I overheard a guy saying that he wanted to get a bet down on a horse. I came over and told him to give it to me, and that I'd get it down with my dad. It was a pretty good bet—$20—and I thought I'd done Dad a favor.

I phoned Dad with the bet, and he got sore at me. "Never do that again!" he shouted. "Forget about gambling and take care of your job and your basketball." We'd never talked much about what I'd do when I grew up, but we kind of assumed that I'd go to college, and then take up some kind of a profession. (By the way, the guy's horse lost, so at least Dad wasn't out any money.)

I came home intending to go to Long Island University, which had good basketball teams then, but the army drafted me instead. They sent me to Fort Sill, Oklahoma, to be a mule-packer with the artillery. We had to break down artillery pieces and pack them onto mules. Some of the pieces weighed 100 pounds or more, and if you didn't put them on just right, the mule would kick you. It was a job for big, strong guys. They wouldn't take you in the unit unless you were at least five feet ten inches tall and weighed more than 180 pounds.

The training was hard, but I liked the army real well. I played a lot of basketball there. I was shipped to Japan, and since the war was over and they didn't need me to pack mules, I went into the military police. I liked that, too. I saw the Orient and had some fun. It wasn't a bad two years.

When I came out of the army, I went to Long Island University on a basketball scholarship. I didn't stay there long. The school was in Brooklyn, and it was just a bunch of buildings with no campus life. I switched to John Marshall College in Jersey City, New Jersey. It was closer to my home, but it was no better. The University of Miami, in Florida, offered me a basketball scholarship, so I headed south.

I loved Miami, but their basketball program was low-key, and the coach wasn't the greatest. I quit after a couple of practices, but I stayed at the school. I was getting G.I. benefits, and a bunch of other ex-G.I.'s there and I got together and rented a house. We didn't bother much with classes—it was tough to go back to being a student after you'd been overseas and all—but we had one heckuva time partying. I think that between us we dated just about every good-looking girl in south Florida.

We hung around the horse and dog tracks and the jai-alai games, and, naturally, did some betting. I had a gambling background, so I took charge of the handicapping. I worked out a system on the dogs that did all right. We also did well betting with the other students on football. Miami played a very tough schedule—teams like Florida, Alabama, Kentucky, and Vanderbilt—but the fraternity boys would bet on Miami no matter what the price. I have to admit that we took advantage of them. For all that, though, we usually were tapped out at least a week before our next check would come from the government. We spent whatever we made, and then some.

My college days ended in 1951, when my dad became ill. My family wasn't wealthy, and I had to go home to handle the business. Believe me, Dad didn't like it that I was running the book like he did. He and Mom had other plans for me. But with him going in and out of the veterans' hospital, and no money coming in, we didn't have much choice.

I didn't mind it at all. I had a high IQ, but school was never for me, and I was glad to be my own man with my own income. With my love of sports, and the taste of winning bets that I got in Florida, I was ready for the action life.

My dad was a solid, conservative man who played it straight with everybody, but I was a young wiseguy, looking to score. I started taking bigger wagers than Dad took, and not turning all of them in to the mob that was running the town. I'd made some friends in Jersey City and New York, and pretty soon I was handling money on "hot" horses from some of the big-time gamblers who didn't want to bet at the tracks because it would knock down their odds, and who had to spread their money around the books so as not to raise too many suspicions. I'd turn those bets over to the local mob and keep the "soft" stuff—the bets from the neighborhood factory workers who mostly lost—for myself. It wasn't long before the boys found me out and tried to do something about it. They set me up for a police bust.

Fortunately, I'd grown up with some of the Union City police and they were my friends. A couple of them warned me what was coming. They told me to get rid of all my gambling material, and I did. When the raiders showed up at the little apartment above the store that I used for an office, they didn't find a thing—almost. It seems that a couple of days before, I'd bought a ticket for the Irish Sweepstakes, and put it in my coat pocket. The cops searched me and found it. They didn't have anything else on me, so they charged me with playing an illegal lottery, which the Irish Sweepstakes was. I was convicted and fined $200. That was my first conviction, and my last for almost 30 years.

I wasn't stupid, and I got the message. From then on, I

was more careful in dealing with the local Mob. Also, at about that same time, I was getting bored hanging around our little candy store in Jersey. I began going to New York more, hanging around with the Broadway "sports" and gambling more and more heavily. After my dad died in 1955, I closed the store and I moved to New York full time.

Now, you have to understand that the gambling scene then wasn't anything like it is today. The National Football League had only 12 teams and played a 12-game regular-season schedule. The National Basketball Association was just getting started, and cities like Syracuse, Rochester, and Fort Wayne were in it. The big sports were baseball—the old, 16-team major leagues—college basketball and football, and boxing.

This was before television sports like we know them now, and before newspapers had the kind of wraparound sports coverage that so many do today. Colleges mostly played local schedules and got local coverage. New York people followed St. John's, New York University, Fordham, and Manhattan College in basketball. They didn't know much about Ohio State or UCLA. Information on games and teams was a lot harder to come by than it is now, and a lot more valuable.

To give you an example of what I mean, I remember a game involving Wilt Chamberlain's University of Kansas team in 1956 or 1957. Kansas was playing Oklahoma A&M and was favored to win by 9 or 10 points. I got a call from a gambling buddy who was plugged in to some big money. He told me that Chamberlain had been hurt and was going to miss the game.

Well, I got about all the money I had and started getting it down on Oklahoma A&M. The game dropped to 8, 7, 6, and 5 points, but I kept betting. I think I put $5,000 on it. I recall that the game went into overtime, and that Kansas may have won, but I collected. It was my biggest win to that point, and it couldn't have happened today. The news of an injury to a player like Chamberlain—a center who stood seven feet two inches tall—would have been all over the country in minutes, and the point spread would have reflected it just as fast, if the game wasn't taken off the books altogether.

The fifties were a very dishonest time for sports. The college basketball point-shaving scandals involving City College of New York and Long Island University came out in 1950 and 1951, but that wasn't the end of that sort of thing by any means. The talk around Lindy's, Stage Delicatessen, and the House of Sports—the restaurants where the gamblers hung out—was usually about basketball games being fixed, although a lot of that was fabricated.

Those also were the days when Jim Norris' International Boxing Club ran boxing, and it later came out in court trials that plenty of boxing matches weren't on the square. Gangsters like Frankie Carbo ran fighters—even champions. In boxing, it didn't do much good to study fighters' records when their matches came up. You had to know which way the fix was going.

I was never involved in any kind of fix, but I was part of the gambling scene in New York then, and I knew a lot of the characters. I knew some big bookies—guys like Champ Nobart, Benny Kaye, and Dave Schwartzberg. And I knew Jack Molinas, who was involved in fixing some college games.

Molinas had played basketball at Columbia University, and later played in the pros. He had access to a lot of the college basketball locker rooms. He'd get close to the kids and find out what it took to buy them. Usually it didn't take much. Professional basketball was just starting then and was no big thing. He'd tell players that if they ever wanted to make a buck on basketball they'd better do it right away. That was his line.

I never liked Molinas. He was a very aggressive person who had no respect for anyone. He double-crossed a lot of guys on the street, and had to leave New York after the fixing scandal hit. He went to California, and was shot and killed in some argument over the porno-films business. People in New York thought he'd end up like that.

It was illegal to be a gambler and bookmaker in New York then—like it is now—but I didn't think I was doing anything terrible. I wasn't part of "organized crime." Disorganized crime, maybe, but never the organized kind.

I've always thought that this country's gambling laws are ridiculous. People have been gambling since the Beginning, and they'll always continue to do so. Churches run Bingo, states run lotteries, and horse and dog tracks operate in just about every state of the United States. New York City has off-track horse-betting parlors all over town. Gambling on every sport you can think of is legal in England, which is certainly a civilized country. But in every state of the United States except Nevada, you can't place a legal wager on a football, baseball, or basketball game or a boxing match.

I don't think that gambling should be pushed down anybody's throat. If the voters of a state don't want gambling legalized, then they shouldn't have it. But I can't think of any reason that someone in, say, Chicago, shouldn't be able to open a betting account in one of the Nevada bookmaking establishments and phone in his wagers from wherever he happens to be. You could make it so he couldn't bet more than he'd put up in cash, so there would be no problems with collections or with compulsive gamblers running up huge tabs that they couldn't cover. If gambling were opened up like that, I think you'd get big companies—maybe the insurance companies—running it. They're very good at setting odds. Also, think of all the taxes that the government could collect. I got tired of being illegal, so I moved to Las Vegas. But I'm getting ahead of myself.

Back in New York as a young man, I wasn't nearly as smart or successful as I am today. I was into gambling pretty heavily and I won quite a bit. But I didn't know my limits, and whatever I'd win, I'd quickly blow on women or horses or games I didn't know anything about. Even with the fixes it was hard to stay ahead, because for every game or fight that you'd get in on right, there would be two or three that would be touted as sure things that were anything but. That was the way most gambling was in those days. Guys, including me, would be trying to read between the lines instead of paying attention to the numbers that were on the paper.

I was broke plenty of times in New York. When I first played there, my dad bailed me out, but later I had to do it myself. Luckily, I got on the right side of one of the biggest loan sharks in the city, and he would stand up for me for nothing.

The guy was Ruby Stein and he was, you know, mob connected. He booked bets, too, and one time, when I was at his hangout, a haberdashery store on the West Side, he gave me a bundle of money to deliver to another bookmaker. He shoved the package at me and said, "Here's ten thousand dollars. Take it to so-and-so."

I took it, went to my car, and I counted it. It turned out that he gave me $20,000, not $10,000. I went back into the store and returned the extra $10,000. Boy, was he surprised and pleased! He said, "Kid, don't ever worry again, because if you need money, you've got it, without the vigorish. Just ask me." And believe me, I asked him plenty of times.

I guess that about the next best thing that happened to me in New York was getting caught by the law. It's funny, but it's true. I made my headquarters in the old Mayflower Hotel on Central Park West and Sixty-first Street. I made my own bets from there, and moved some money for other people. This was in the late 1950s, and the Feds were hot on everybody's trail. Telephones all over town were tapped, including mine, I was to learn.

The case I got involved in was one of the biggest of the time. The key figure was Leo Shaefer. He was a big bookie—a really big one. He'd done business in Chicago and Canada, but his base at the time was Terre Haute, Indiana. He had lines out to bookies and players all over the United States.

People would call Leo in Terre Haute to place bets and to lay off money. I never did either of those things. I was doing some pretty good handicapping on professional basketball at the time, and the Shaefer people would call me to ask my opinion about various betting lines. When the taps were in, my name and voice came up. The Feds made their case and subpoenaed maybe 300 players to testify about their involvement with the Shaefer bunch. I was one of them.

I was 30 years old then, and I think I was the youngest guy caught up in that case. The others were old-timers and big, big gamblers. Ray Ryan was one, and so was one of the Marx brothers in New York (they were gamblers, not comedians). A lot of the big bookmakers around the country got involved. I knew a few of the defendants, but not very well.

This was a grand jury hearing, and while I was at home waiting to be called to testify, Leo Shaefer telephoned me. He said, "You're a young fellow. Don't get yourself in trouble for me. Tell the truth. If you don't want to tell the truth, take the Fifth Amendment." The Fifth Amendment is the one against self-incrimination. It was very popular back then. I talked to a lawyer, and he thought that taking the Fifth was a good idea. When I was called to testify, that was what I did.

I suppose I could have got in trouble for that, but it was such a big trial, and there were so many more important guys than me involved, that the government never pursued me further. Meantime, in hanging around the courthouse waiting to be called, I met Sid Wyman, who was to have a big influence on my life.

Sid was one of the top gambling people in the country then. At one time he owned the Riviera Hotel in Las Vegas, and another time he had a major interest in the

Dunes. Sid was a very substantial guy. He was a top card player. He was a good casino player. He played very high in sports. He taught me about shopping the books for prices—about how to get the most for your money. I never thanked him enough for that.

During the grand jury hearings, and the trial in Indianapolis that followed, Sid and I got to be good friends. On weekends, we'd fly into Cincinnati and visit the casinos in Newport, Kentucky. We had some good times.

Sid took a liking to me and thought I was smart. He told me that I was wasting my time dodging the law trying to get bets down in New York. He said he'd set me up in Las Vegas, where gambling was legal, if I moved out there.

Sid wanted me to run a book called the Saratoga. It was at 114 South First Street in downtown Las Vegas. I'd never been to Vegas before then, but I went to look around. A lot of people are turned off by the hot desert climate, but I liked it. I'd seldom had a suntan before I came to Nevada, but I haven't been without one since. There's nothing like looking healthy.

I moved to Las Vegas with the idea of going into business with Sid and making a living behind the counter. The trouble was, Sid was having financial troubles at the time, and so was Irwin Gordon, another one of the owners of the place. I wound up with a betting parlor but no bankroll. I tried to make a go of it with some money I'd saved, but I couldn't swing it. We got to the point where we were paying off Monday's winners with the bets we took in on Tuesday. That couldn't last, and it didn't. I think we got through one baseball season before we closed.

By that time, though, I was committed to Las Vegas, and something else good had happened to me: I fell in love. The girl was Delores Vicario, who called herself Debbie because she didn't like the name Delores. We immediately had something in common: neither of us liked the first names we had been given.

I'd met Debbie a couple of years before in New Jersey.

She lived there with her family, which was Italian, and worked as a model in New York's garment district. I met her through a union official I knew. I'd given him a few winners, and he wanted to reciprocate. He said he knew a real beautiful girl and wanted to fix me up with her. I said, "Sure."

On our first date, I took her to Monmouth Park racetrack on the Jersey Shore. We had a great time. Besides being pretty, she was smart and fun to be with, and she liked me a lot. I'd had enough of showgirls and strippers by then, and was ready to settle down. When she said she'd come to Las Vegas, I asked her to marry me. We were married in Las Vegas on April 11, 1959, and we've been together since. I think we're the longest-married couple in town.

I was almost 32 years old when I got married, but I think it made an adult of me for the first time. There's something about making a living as a gambler that keeps you immature. Before then, I'd never worried much about money. If I had it, I spent it. If I needed it, I'd borrow, and figure out how to pay it back later.

I can't claim that I shook off that way of life overnight. As I've told you, I was almost broke on the night of January 27, 1960, when my daughter, Blaine, was born, and I had to cash a couple of basketball bets to pay the hospital bills. But I was getting better.

Having to support a wife and child made me remember some of the things my father told me when I was a kid. He never told it like a lecture, but he gave it to me a little at a time when we were at the fights or a ballgame, or together at night in the candy store tallying up the day's receipts.

He told me not to bet what I'd like to win, but what I could afford to lose. That's the best advice I've ever received. He said that the harder a person works, the luckier he gets. He said that when someone gets behind, he shouldn't try to get even all at once, but a little at a time.

He said that tomorrow was another day, and that a gambler on a losing streak was like a baseball player in a hitting slump. The ball player would go to his batting coach for advice. The coach would tell him, "Don't swing from the heels. Choke up on the bat and just try to make contact. Whack the ball up the middle. The hits will start coming." Whenever I go into losing streaks—and, believe me, I have them—I think of that advice and it helps.

My dad first taught me the wisdom of going against public opinion, which is the essence of my betting style today. When we would go to the horse races, he'd look for horses that had been beaten as favorites and were dropping down in class. People would see their poor performance in the *Racing Form,* and ignore the fact that they were in against poorer company and were carrying less weight than they had before. He got a lot of bargains that way. He said it was the law of supply and demand in action, just like they taught in school. He used to say that prices on December 26 are always lower than on December 24. I think of that line almost every day.

This is not to say that getting married turned me into an instant winner. That's not the way things work. Gambling still was, and is, a tough business. I was on the edge and betting my last dollars plenty of times after I'd settled down.

Once, in 1964, I'd had a particularly bad run of luck and was thinking about packing it in and finally getting a straight job. I'd win one bet and lose two, win two and lose three. Just when I thought I was getting a bit ahead, I'd slide back again.

But I think that one game proved to be a turning point for me. It came at the end of the 1964 football season, and matched Notre Dame against the University of Southern California.

Notre Dame came into that game undefeated with one of their best teams ever. John Huarte was their quarterback and Jack Snow was his top receiver. Nick Eddy was a great running back for them. Alan Page anchored their defensive line.

Southern Cal had a good team, too. Mike Garrett was their tailback—he'd win the Heisman Trophy the following year—and Craig Fertig was their quarterback. Also, they were getting back for the Notre Dame game some players who'd been out with injuries earlier in the year.

Notre Dame always gets a lot of gambling support wherever it plays, and this game was no exception. The teams were playing at the Los Angeles Coliseum, Southern Cal's home field, but Notre Dame opened as an 8-point betting favorite and quickly went to 10 points. I had the game figured as no worse than even. Breaking all my rules of money management, I took about all the money I had at the time—almost $10,000—and put it on Southern Cal plus the 10 points. I figured that if I won I'd stay in business as a gambler, and if I lost I'd try something else. With the few bucks I had left, I bought a half-dozen of the best seats in the Coliseum, hired a limousine, and invited some friends to go to the game as my guests. If I was going out, I was going out in style.

The first half of that game couldn't have been worse for me. Southern Cal did everything but score. They marched up and down the field, but every time they got close to the end zone, they fumbled or had a pass intercepted. Meantime, everything Notre Dame did was golden. They took advantage of every opportunity, and led 17–0 at the half.

I don't usually eat hotdogs or anything else at football halftimes, but that afternoon I went to a concession stand and bought one, just to get away from the people I was with. I was really down. While I was chewing, though, I overheard people saying that it was the closest 17–0 game they'd ever seen and that with a break or two Southern Cal could get back in it.

I went back to my seat feeling better, and the people I overheard turned out to be right. Southern Cal scored 20 unanswered points in the second half to win, 20–17. I pocketed my winnings and went on to have a great November and December betting on the pros. I've never been close to broke since.

As the years went by my reputation grew, and the press started paying attention to me. I've always liked sportswriters, and I talk to them about their local teams whenever I get the chance. Some of them started calling me for my picks on different games, and printing them in their papers. *Sports Illustrated* magazine interviewed me, and so did some of the television networks. I was mentioned in some books on gambling, including Larry Merchant's *National Football Lottery,* a very good one. My name was getting around.

Starting in 1972, I picked the winner of 13 straight professional football Super Bowl games, with every pick documented in the newspapers. A few of those picks were guesses and pure luck—I never expect to go 13 of 13 in any sport—but they also helped my reputation. I was asked to do a football-betting column in the *Las Vegas Review-Journal,* and, at various times, in the *New York Post,* New York *Daily News, Chicago Tribune,* and *San Francisco Chronicle.* I never took any pay for those columns; I thought of them as a public service, helping to give the average-guy bettor a better chance against the bookies. The *Daily News* insisted on paying me, so I turned their checks over to charity.

I'd become a solid citizen and thought my troubles were behind me, but then the Feds popped up to give me a nasty surprise. I think that how it happened says a lot about the mess that this country's gambling laws are in.

In the late 1970s, I met a fellow around the casinos who called himself Johnny Bryan, but whose real name was John Baborian. I met him like I meet a lot of people: he was a guy I'd see around the casinos from time to time and talk sports with. He asked me who I liked, I asked him who he liked. Eventually, we got to be closer and our wives became friendly. He told me he was from Rhode Island, but he also said he had an apartment in Las Vegas, and I saw him around town so much that I figured that he'd moved here.

One day in 1978 there was a knock on my door, and four men were standing outside with a warrant to search my house. They were from the Federal Bureau of Investigation. I asked them why they were after me. They said I was a suspect in a gambling investigation.

I had no choice, so I let them in. A couple of them were pretty nasty. We owned three dogs then, and they were as tame as can be, but one of them barked at an FBI guy and he threatened to shoot the dog if he barked again. They scrambled through the whole house, opening drawers and looking into closets. They treated me like I was Public Enemy Number One.

It turned out that they had got my voice on tape talking from Las Vegas to Johnny Bryan in Providence, Rhode Island. He was part of a gambling operation the Feds were watching there. He'd called me one day during the football season, and since I'd seen him in Las Vegas just a few days before that, I assumed he was calling from here.

He was interested in who I liked in a Pittsburgh Steelers game. I said I liked the Steelers and had taken them with 6 points. I forget who they were playing. He said he wished he could get 6 points on that game. I said he should hold on, and I'd see if I could get it for him. I picked up my other phone and called the book in town where I'd made my bet. I asked if they were still giving the 6. They said yes. I got on the other phone and told Bryan that he was on. I didn't take the bet myself. I just placed it for him at a legal bookmaking place. I never thought twice about it.

But when the case came to trial in Rhode Island, I was a defendant. They charged me with using interstate communications facilities—my phone—to transmit gambling information, which is against federal law. I had to hire a lawyer (two, actually), make six trips to Rhode Island for consultations and court appearances, and bring in character witnesses to testify on my behalf. It cost me plenty.

I think that by the end of the trial the judge was convinced I'd gotten dragged into the case unfairly, but I had talked to Bryan about point spreads on the telephone between Rhode Island and Las Vegas, and, like I said, that's against the law. I was fined $10,000 and given 2 years' probation. It was my first conviction since that $200 fine in New Jersey for having an Irish Sweepstakes ticket.

The fine was no big deal and I also could handle my legal costs, but I was still embarrassed by the whole thing. Some of the editors who ran my newspaper columns felt funny about carrying them while I was on probation, so I stopped writing them. That was too bad, because I enjoyed doing the columns.

I think it's stupid that a mere telephone conversation about football point spreads—which just about every big-city sports page carries these days—is a federal offense. There's definitely something wrong with a law like that. It should be changed.

That case, though, had no effect on my gambling, and the last few years have been the best I've ever had. I consider myself very lucky to be able to earn a living—and a nice one—doing something I love. Sports betting is a fascinating occupation, and it's just as interesting as a hobby. I hope the information to come helps you get more out of yours.

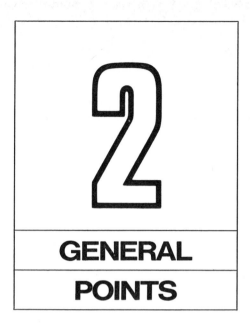

GENERAL
POINTS

I could start out with a lot of technical stuff about power ratings and opponent evaluations, but I think it's important that a gambler begin with a clear general idea of what he's up to. In my case, it's making a living, so I look at gambling the way an engineer looks at a bridge. I assume that, for most of you, betting is a hobby—a way to increase your enjoyment of the games you watch. You don't want to build the bridge, just get across it to where you're going. This dictates a different approach.

I don't recommend that anyone take up gambling as a livelihood. It's far too difficult for that. As I said in the previous chapter, it took me almost 20 years to earn a reliable income from it. I stuck with it because I liked the life and always was lucky enough to win when I had to. In the latter experience, I'm definitely the exception, not the rule.

How hard is it to win year in and year out? For starters, you have to be right 52.38 percent of the time to *break even* against the standard bookmakers' odds of 11 to 10 in football and basketball. That's tougher than it looks. To be right 55 percent of the time over the long haul—about what it takes to be solidly in the black—the odds are roughly 6 to 1 against you.

Professional football is the most popular game to bet on because there are relatively few teams (28), their personnel are well known, and news of their activities is easy to come by. Yet according to Mort Olshan, whose Los Angeles-based *Gold Sheet* is the country's oldest and best football service, between 35 and 40 percent of all pro-football betting underdogs have won their games *straight up* in recent seasons, which means that the bookmakers and the public make the wrong favorite almost half the time.

Mort also reports that, for the seasons 1979–1980 through 1984–1985, the pro-football teams that beat the point spread most often were the San Francisco 49ers with a 50-win, 30-loss record, followed by the Miami Dolphins at 49 and 31. Not as impressive as you'd think, is it? It means that, even if you got on the best bandwagons around, you would have lost almost 4 of every 10 bets you placed.

Las Vegas is a good place from which to view the losers of the world, and I've seen plenty of them. I've seen successful men get the gambling bug and wind up losing their businesses, their homes, and their wives, although a few times that last thing wasn't so bad.

I'll never forget the time that a guy who had a reputation around town as being a successful gambler knocked on my door and asked to borrow some money so he could pay his rent. I gave it to him, and was surprised to learn the next day that he'd just put a thousand bucks on a prizefight. The next time I saw him I asked him what was going on. He said, "Oh, I've got some money to bet with. I just came up short on my bills." That's the kind of degenerate thinking that gambling produces.

The main reason that sports gamblers bite the dust isn't because they are dumb, but because they underestimate the complexity of the activity. Sports are contested by humans, and humans make mistakes. If every offensive player on a football team carried out his assignment like his coach wanted him to, every play would go for a touchdown, but you know how often that happens. In baseball, a pitcher is throwing a 90-mile-an-hour fastball and a batter is trying to hit it with a rounded club. One-hundredth of an inch on the bat can be the difference between a home run and an easy fly ball. That's the kind of proposition the sports gambler must deal with. Keeping that in mind should help you keep your betting in perspective.

BEING A FAN

One place where the professional gambler and the average-guy bettor part company is on being a fan. A pro gambler can't afford to be one. By definition, a fan has an emotional attachment to a team, and he sticks with it through thick and thin. To be successful in gambling, you have to analyze things objectively. A gambler's favorite team is the one that just won a bet for him.

I won't say that I never root. If I'm watching a game and have no money on it, I'll usually pull for the underdog or the team that's been playing poorly, just like most people. But that's as far as I go. A fan is always looking for reasons to make his team win, and that's not the approach that produces winning bets. You have to look at the bad as well as the good. If you can't always do that—and if they are honest with themselves, most people will recognize that they can't—either you shouldn't bet on teams you root for or you should keep your wagers on them small.

Rooting can hurt bettors in more direct ways. If a bookmaker gets to know your preference, he'll try to make you pay for it. If he knows, for instance, that you're a New York Giants fan in football, and he has the Giants by 6 points in a certain game, he may ask you to lay 6½ or even 7 points to get down on your team. He'll sometimes do that if you get into a pattern of betting on particular teams even if you don't root for them in an emotional way.

In some areas of the country, *all* the bookies jack up their spreads to make it expensive for the home folks to back their favorites. If the University of Nebraska is a 17-point Las Vegas favorite in a football game, it may be as much as a 20-point choice in Lincoln, Nebraska. That even happens in some bigger towns.

There are a couple of ways to beat that sort of point padding by the bookies. The most obvious way—and the most effective—is to make the *bookie* pay by going against local sentiment and taking the other team. Another way is to shop for a better price on your team, although I understand that not everyone is in a position to do that.

It's important that, when you're inquiring about the point spreads from the person you bet with, you don't tip your hand. Instead of saying, "Gimme the Detroit Lions game," just ask for the day's rundown in whatever order he wants to give it. Asking for a particular team can be a tipoff that you want to bet on it.

WATCHING GAMES

Most of us get to be fans—and bettors—because we like watching sports and the excitement they bring us. Watching games with bets in mind, however, should be different from watching them simply for fun. Unless a gambler can get halftime bets down, and Las Vegas is the only place I know of where you can do that, he already has made his plays when the games begin. He watches for what they can tell him about tomorrow's action, or the next weekend's. He watches to get a clearer view of both teams—let me repeat that: *both* teams—than he can get from reading about the game in his newspaper the next morning.

Some people play the stock market by shutting out all the "fundamental" factors that make stocks move, such as company profits and industry trends, and concentrating solely on the movement of the prices of individual issues. These people are called "technicians." They operate in a theoretically closed room into which nothing save their stock-price figures can intrude. Some people gamble like that, too. They refuse on principle to watch any games, judging teams solely by their statistics.

I'm not that way, but there's something to be said for that approach. Too often you can get a distorted notion about a team by watching it play, especially if its performance in the game you happen to see is unusually good or unusually bad. Furthermore, statistics can give a picture of a team that is quite adequate for a betting judgment. I make plenty of bets on teams I've never watched, particularly in college basketball, where there are so many teams that it's impossible to see them all.

However, as I've said, I do watch a lot of games. In fact, I spent $8,000 for a television satellite dish that can bring in stations from almost anywhere in the United States. On football weekends, I'll often watch three or four college games and as many pro games, sometimes several at a time.

Ninety-nine percent of the time, I watch games on television—not in person—because I can see them better on the home screen. I enjoy going to the stadium as much as the next guy, but there's no beating the seat that TV gives you, not to mention the replays. Most of the time, after you've gone to a game, you have to have a friend who saw it on the tube describe the key plays to you.

I think that football is the best television game by far. The replays isolate the important action and show clearly who did what to whom among 22 players on the field at any given time. Baseball is next best: the standard camera shot that shows pitcher, batter, and catcher from center field gives you a better look at what the pitcher is throwing than any but a handful of seats at the ballpark. And, watching at home, the beer is cheaper.

I watch to see how the game is played, not just how it turns out. In football, especially the college kind, I look first at the strengths of the two teams where it counts most: on the lines. Usually, the team that controls the line of scrimmage controls the game, so I want to see who is doing the most pushing. The team that rules the ground doesn't always win or cover; a good passing game alone sometimes will suffice. Also, sometimes a good running team gets behind and must pass more than it wants to in order to catch up. But strength on the ground still counts for the most in my book.

I watch football to see if the final score accurately reflects how the game was played. Maybe you'll notice in your newspaper that one team beats another by 21 points, and you'll put it down as a romp. What you might not know is that the winner was up by only one touchdown in the late going, but twice scored quickly on turnovers because the trailing team got incautious while trying to catch up. The real difference between the teams was one touchdown, not three.

It can work the other way, too. A team with, say, a 10-point lead sometimes will go into one of those "prevent" defenses in the late going, giving its opponent short-pass completions in bounds to keep the clock running. The team may give up a lot of yards that way, and its final margin may be cut to 3 points. But that won't have been the real difference between it and its opponent. Quite a few bargains will come your way if you can tell a game's real score from the one on the scoreboard when the final gun sounds.

I also watch to get a reading on teams' emotional states. Is a football team playing with fire and determination, or just going through the motions? Are a baseball team's infielders diving for balls or just waving at them as they go through? Is a basketball coach substituting with a purpose, or just running players in and out of a game in the hope that someone might do something good? Are the home-team's fans a factor, or do they sit on their hands? This information can come only from watching.

I watch college basketball games to see how teams handle the ball, and whether the refereeing played a major role in the outcome. The ball-handling part is especially important when good teams play one another. I'll watch a good team—say, Georgetown or Duke—play a lesser opponent to see what it does with the ball in the final minutes when it is ahead. That won't be as big a factor as it was before the 1985–1986 season, when the 45-second shot clock became universal in college basketball. But if I know that a team can run out the clock when it's ahead against a mediocre opponent, I'll be more likely to pick it when it runs into a strong foe.

Refereeing can have a big impact on a basketball game, and this is rarely reflected in newspaper accounts. I think it's safe to say that foul calls make the difference in 15 or 20 percent of all college games, with the home team getting the best of it maybe two-thirds of the time. Knowing that a team won or lost a game because of referee's calls is as valuable a piece of information as a gambler can have.

It's important to watch games with your eyes and not your ears. If you're an astute observer—and you have to be one to succeed as a bettor—you'll see things on your television screen that the announcers won't mention. Much of the sports announcing on television today is merely public relations for the home team. Baseball and basketball announcers are rarely critical of the teams they cover because the team, not the station that carries the games, pays their salaries. In football, the announcers work for the networks, but the National Football League and the National Collegiate Athletic Association have the right to approve them, which pretty much puts the announcers in their pockets.

Sometimes, the rules that teams make for their broadcasters are pretty ridiculous. I remember reading where the late Bill Veeck, who used to own the Chicago White Sox, once bawled out one of his radio announcers for mentioning that it was cold at the ballpark on a particular night. Veeck told the guy that it's *never* cold at the ballpark.

There are, however, some broadcasters who are worth listening to because of the insights they can provide. It's my opinion that ex-players usually make poor broadcasters because they don't want to get their old playing buddies sore at them, but there are exceptions. Steve Stone, the former pitcher who helps Harry Caray do the Chicago Cubs games on television, is great at telling what pitches the pitchers for both teams are using effectively, and Tom Seaver has done the same thing on some of the postseason games he has done for the TV networks.

John Madden, the former Oakland Raiders football coach, is excellent at explaining the psychology of football players and teams, and pointing out which players like to stick their noses in it and which don't. I never turn off the sound when he's doing a game.

WHAT TO READ

A bettor has to keep up on sports by reading, and that isn't too hard these days. Indeed, with sports coverage being as extensive as it is, the main problem is limiting what you read.

A daily newspaper that covers sports broadly is a must, and just about every big city has one. In Las Vegas, I follow both papers, the *Sun* and the *Review-Journal.* They carry all the standings and statistics of the sports in season.

If your town's newspaper doesn't have good sports coverage, get *USA Today,* which does. In fact, I think that *USA Today* has one of the best sports sections anywhere. It gives you a little about everything, and while it doesn't have the in-depth coverage of individual teams that most metropolitan dailies have, I think that *USA Today*'s cover-the-map system might be better for the person interested in gambling. It also gives you very reliable odds and point spreads on sports.

There are other publications that the fan-bettor can use for information. The weekly *Sporting News* isn't betting oriented, but it goes into more detail on the major sports than any other newspaper. I particularly like the gossip-type columns it runs; what player doesn't get along with what coach, and that sort of thing. A lot of times I find myself taking that kind of information into account when I'm planning my bets.

Sports Illustrated magazine is nicely written, but its articles are long and it contains too much stuff about sports like sailing and hunting that I'm not interested in. The same goes for *Inside Sports* magazine.

Some bettors who follow college football and basketball make a thing out of reading all the recruiting publications that have come on the market in the last few years, but I leave them alone. First, there are too many of them to keep up with. Second, a lot of the kids they write about never wind up being a factor for the colleges that sign them. And if they do get to be stars, I'll have plenty of chances to read about them later. Third, most of them are written so far in advance of the season that a lot of their information is out of date before you read it.

COMPUTERS

You hear a lot today about how people use computers to help them handicap sports. I keep myself open to new developments in this field, but based on what I've seen I don't think they help much.

The biggest limitation of computers is that they can only tell you what happened in the past—not what's going to happen. They can't account for the emotional states of teams and the possible consequences of injuries to players.

And they are of very little help in any sport in the early weeks of a new season, when there aren't enough current numbers to feed them.

Computers can spew out statistics in great volume, but, as far as I'm concerned, that's as much of a hindrance as a help. The problem for us sports fans today is *too much* information to go through. Computers can be a handy way to summon up data that can be cumbersome to store by hand, and they can crank out ratios that bettors can use, but you can do that latter thing with a calculator. That's what I do, and I think I save money that way. But like I say, I'm always ready to be shown otherwise.

TOUT SHEETS

One sort of publication there is no shortage of—unfortunately—is the tout sheet. These are the outfits that promise to give you betting winners for a price. In my opinion, 99 percent of them are pure garbage. They are put out by guys who went broke gambling with their own money, and now are trying it with yours.

It's a mystery to me how the gambling laws let the tout sheets operate. Some of them advertise in publications that circulate all around the country, and the ESPN national cable television network even carried their ads for a while. A lot of them have 800 telephone numbers. Yet they don't get arrested for sending gambling information across state lines. Their defense is that the information they pass out is "news." That's news to me, and to a lot of other people.

Tout sheets have been operating in this country for decades, and they use the same scams over and over. You'll see ones advertise that they'll only make you pay them if they give you a winner. You'll get one game from them and lose, get another and lose, and, maybe, finally, get one that wins. They'll collect on the winner, and the losers don't cost them a dime. Some bargain!

Some of the sheets run five or six services with different names, and they'll pass their customers around between them. Say you sign up with one service and it doesn't do you any good, so you quit. Right away you'll get a call from a salesman. "How'd you like your last service?" the guy will ask. You'll say "lousy" and he'll be sympathetic. "Hey," he'll say. "We've been doing great. Why not sign up with us?" So you sign up, only you'll be giving your money to the same people who cheated you before.

I've known dozens of guys who've run tout sheets, and I've been impressed with very few of them. Some of them do things like fix cars and wait on tables for a living. I remember seeing one sheet run an ad showing its owner with a patch over one eye. The next year it advertised again, and the patch was over his other eye.

There was even a sheet run by Johnny Unitas, the old Baltimore Colts quarterback. I didn't follow it, and maybe Unitas does know how to figure games, but if he does he's one of the few jocks or ex-jocks who can. There's a saying around the horse-race tracks that a guy could get rich if he had the jockeys' betting concession, and my observation is that that's true of athletes in other sports, too. You'll recall that Art Schlichter, the former Indianapolis Colts quarterback, got in trouble for losing something like $1 million on bets and not being able to pay. I wasn't surprised that he lost. I was surprised that anybody would let him run up a tab that large.

Danny Sheridan made a big name for himself in the tout-sheet business; a lot of newspapers call him for his opinions about games. I've never tracked his service but I met him once, and my eyebrows went up when he told me that he never bet. As far as I'm concerned, someone who doesn't gamble has no business advising people who do. That's like the Pope telling people how to run their sex lives. If you don't play the game, you have no business making the rules.

Gary Austin is another fellow who made a name for

himself as a sheet operator. He was a real estate salesman who won a football-betting contest run by the Castaways Sports Book one year, and got a lot of publicity out of it. The next thing you knew, he'd opened his own service. He had a good business head, and the sheet did well. But as soon as he could afford it, Austin closed it and opened his own sports book on the Las Vegas Strip. He did okay there for a couple of years, but went out of business in the fall of 1985. I hope he gets things together again, because he owes me a few dollars.

The second year Austin was in the business, he approached me about him putting out a service under my name. He wasn't the first guy who ever asked me about that, but he was the only one I ever really listened to. He had all the equipment, the secretaries, and the guys who would help keep statistics for me. He offered me a very nice piece of change, win or lose.

I thought about it but said no. I told him that, in the first place, I'd insist on being honest about how I was doing, and because of that I wouldn't be able to compete with all these phonies who claim to pick 75 or 80 percent winners. Also, I have my bad weeks, and I'd hate to think that anybody else paid money to lose with me. That's another reason I never accept money for doing my newspaper betting columns, although, fortunately, I never had anything to apologize for there. Anybody who followed my picks in any of the years I wrote for the papers would have come out nicely ahead. You can look that up.

There are a couple of exceptions to my low opinion of sports-betting services. One is Mort Olshan's *Gold Sheet*. Mort has been in the business since 1957. That's far, far longer than anyone else, and that alone should tell you that he's all right. He's a classy and honorable guy who never makes false claims about his record on picks, which, by the way, is usually good. I don't follow Mort's selections because I prefer to make my own. I assume that you do, too, or you wouldn't be reading this book. Still, I think the

Gold Sheet is useful for the statistical information it carries, and I usually find that Mort's power ratings in football and basketball aren't too different from mine.

Another sheet worth following is the *Sports Reporter,* out of Lynbrook, New York. Rich Bomze runs it, and he's knowledgeable. His publication gives you computerized statistical breakdowns by conferences in both college football and college basketball that you can't get elsewhere. Also, it follows a lot of small-college basketball teams that other services don't. That often comes in handy to me around tournament time in that sport.

"LOCKS"

The subject of touts leads me right into "locks," which are games that the bettor supposedly can't lose. Some of the tout services have made names for themselves by picking these games, although it's my observation that they are wrong on them as often as they are right. As far as I'm concerned, the only "locks" that can't miss is spelled with an "x" and goes great with bagels and cream cheese. There are plenty of times during a season when I'll see games I like really well, and I'll bet them accordingly. But I'd never, never be so arrogant as to call them sure things. There's no such animal in betting.

Let me give you a couple of examples. If someone had offered you 21 points and the Miami Dolphins against the San Francisco 49ers in the 1985 Super Bowl, you probably would have mortgaged your house to bet on Miami, but you'd have lost. How about the Washington Redskins and 28 points against the Los Angeles Raiders in the Super Bowl the year before? You'd have lost that one, too.

The way some of the tout services advertise their so-called "lock" games makes them especially suspect. They're out touting them two or three weeks in advance, before the teams' records and injury situations are known, and before they have the faintest idea what the weather will be like on game day. Sure, it doesn't snow much in the West and South during football season, but it can rain, and rain can knock anyone's plans for a loop.

A couple of "lock" games stand out in my mind. One had the University of Texas over Notre Dame in the 1977 Cotton Bowl. Texas had Earl Campbell and a terrific wishbone-formation ground attack that was eating up everybody. One service made Texas the "lock of the century" or some such stupid thing. Notre Dame had a big line and some real good linebackers. The Irish played an almost seven-man line against the Texas wishbone and stacked it up completely. Not only did Texas fail to cover, it failed to win. The score was 38–10.

Another "lock" was Florida over West Virginia in the 1981 Peach Bowl. Florida had a powerful team that year, while West Virginia was supposed to be lucky to get into the game. The betting opened with Florida a 7-point favorite, which I thought was about right. Then one service announced it as a "lock" for Florida, and just about everybody and his cousin jumped in on it. Pretty soon the game was up to 14, and even 14½ in some places!

I'll never forget meeting a fellow outside the Barbary Coast Hotel in Las Vegas late one night the week before that game. He must have recognized me, because he came up, called me by name, and asked me who I liked in that game. I remember that he had his wife and young son with him, even though it was after midnight. I think the spread had gone to 13 on Florida at that point, and I told him to take the points, which I was doing. He seemed shocked. He said, "Lem, don't you know the game is a lock? I'm going heavy on Florida." I could only shake my head and shrug. Here was a poor guy betting his rent money at atrocious points because he'd heard that some tout said he should.

Do I have to tell you what happened? It rained like crazy on the day of the game, and there were an awful lot of turnovers on the grass field, most of them by Florida.

Oliver Luck was playing quarterback for West Virginia—he later played in the pros—and had a heckuva day. West Virginia won the game, 26–6, and so did I.

My strategy on so-called lock games is the same as it is on other games: if you like the points, take the underdog, no matter what some tout says. In fact, he'll often make it a better play for you.

"SMART MONEY"

A lot of times you'll see point spreads or odds move just before a game, and you'll hear that "smart money" caused it. The assumption is that money that's bet late is somehow smarter than money that's bet early. Don't believe it.

I usually bet late on games because that way I protect myself against swings caused by information I don't have. Still, I'm not a subscriber to the "smart money" theory. In fact, if you know how Las Vegas works, it's really just the opposite. Many of the sports books test their lines against top gamblers *early*—before they open them to the public. They give these guys a chance to cop a good bet in return for the information that they obtain from knowing their decisions, and they adjust their spreads accordingly. I know, because I used to get in on that a lot. Some of the line testers bet very little money—as little as $100—but their opinions are worth more than those of guys who bet 100 times as much later.

Smartness isn't what moves the spreads, bigness does, so when you hear "smart money," substitute "big money." Is big money usually right? Not any more often than the smaller stuff. You can be sure that just about all the guys who pull up to bet in Cadillacs earned them in some other occupation.

I watch the late-money moves mainly to see if they push the spreads past certain key numbers. In football, those usually would be 3, 4, 6, 7, or 10 points. Those are the margins by which a lot of games are decided. If I know of no convincing reason for the shift, I'll bet against it.

FIXED GAMES

You hear a lot of rumors about games being fixed, but very, very few of them are true—a lot fewer than you might think. As I've said before, college basketball fixes were pretty common back in the 1950s around New York, but things have changed since then. The rise of the National Basketball Association and the National Football League—and the rise in player salaries—means that more kids have a chance to make big money as pros, and they're not likely to blow it by fooling around with gamblers while they're in college. I think that the 1985 stink involving the Tulane University basketball team should underscore that. One of the kids implicated in that—a center named John Williams—was a pretty good NBA prospect. He pleaded innocent, and was acquitted after two trials. But if he had been found guilty, a promising and lucrative career would have been blown.

People think that we Las Vegas types know all about the fix rumors, but I'm here to tell you that we don't. I wound up on the wrong side of a couple of the games that were mentioned in the Tulane episode. From what I read, a local group in New Orleans was behind it—college kids and some small-time hustlers. You should know that, in a kind of funny way, gambling's being illegal gives the public some added protection against fixed games. Except in Las Vegas, illegal bookmakers handle all the sports action, and they're the ones who are out money when a game isn't right. Some of those boys have been known to get nasty when they think they've been cheated. Anyone who tries a fix will have the "boys" to contend with as well as the cops. Given the choice, I'd rather be on the outs with the cops.

I don't claim to be an expert on the subject, but I think

that fixing a team game would be quite difficult. You'd just about have to involve a star, and a kid with a pro career in sight, or a pro making the kind of huge salaries they pay today, would be very expensive to enlist. And even if the player did sign up, what would keep his coach from pulling him if he went out and played poorly?

Getting enough money down on a fixed game to make it worthwhile would be another problem. No matter what you may read, an extraordinarily large bet from any source raises eyebrows in Las Vegas, and I'd think it'd have an even bigger impact in illegal circles outside Nevada. "Unnatural" money sends out alarms all over. People start asking questions and taking names. It wouldn't be long before a game that's suspect is taken off the board.

That's what foiled one of the few fixed-game schemes that I have any firsthand knowledge of. Some years ago, Bob Martin, one of the smartest odds makers in Las Vegas, called to tell me about something that had come to his attention. He said that a guy who usually bet $500 a game was betting $5,000 a game on professional basketball, and winning. He thought that maybe something funny was up.

Bob and I started to follow this guy's bets. After three or four games it became fairly clear that their common denominator was a referee. Now neither of us had any proof, but we made a few calls and, indirectly, brought our suspicions to the league's attention. Pretty soon, that referee wasn't in the NBA anymore, even though nothing formal was filed against him.

That case makes another point that I think is worth mentioning: if a fix is in, it would just as likely involve a game official as a player. That's especially true in college sports, where the refs are older men who are most likely to understand what's involved in a deal and how to profit from it. But that's just conjecture on my part. As far as I know, the officiating today in the professional leagues and the major college athletic conferences is completely on the up and up.

And that's fortunate because, much more than most people, gamblers have a vested interest in the integrity of sports. All of our careful calculations mean nothing if a game isn't being played squarely. It's tough enough choosing on paper who's the better of two teams without having to wonder if any of the players, coaches, or officials have something up their sleeves.

A FINAL POINT

One last general thing that I want to make clear is the need for gamblers to take occasional breaks from their playing. There's nothing that can get a person staler than watching and figuring sports. They play seven days a week in every season but football, and with all the sports on television it's not uncommon to watch two or three games a night. Pretty soon you'll hear basketballs bouncing or see baseballs being hit in your dreams.

A pro like me has to be particularly careful not to overdo things. I try to set aside one day a week when I don't watch any games. If you have a five-day-a-week job, and you watch and bet on sports seriously the other two, you're working seven days. At least once a month, take a vacation from sports. Take your kids to the zoo or the beach. Take your wife out for dinner. You'll come back better for it, and your family will like you more.

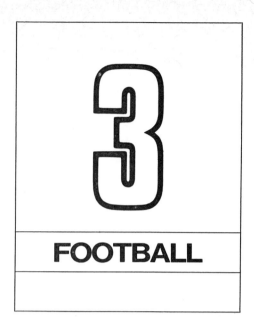

FOOTBALL

Football is the sport I'm most closely associated with in the public's mind because of my newspaper football-betting columns, and it's the one that has been the kindest to me over the years. I think that I've been successful betting on football partly because it's my favorite game to watch. When you like what you're doing, you're more likely to do well at it.

It's kind of funny that I'm so crazy about football, because it wasn't all that big back in the 1930s when I was growing up. The National Football League was around then, but it was strictly an Eastern and Midwestern league with an 11-game schedule, and people didn't pay too much attention to it. College football was the big game, but you have to remember that not many people went to college in those days, so its audience was small compared to today's.

The people in the Union City neighborhood where I lived weren't college types. On autumn Saturdays, they'd be off at the racetrack or home snoozing instead of out cheering for Rutgers or Princeton.

Like I said before, I was tall and skinny as a kid, and basketball was the game I played best. But I also played end on my high school football team. What I learned was that football isn't the caveman type of game that it looks like to people who don't understand it. That included my folks, who were always after me to quit because they were afraid I would get hurt.

Our high school coach was Barney Finn. He'd played his college ball under Lou Little, the famous coach at Columbia University. Finn taught us a couple of the trick plays that Little liked to use. One was the "sleeper play," where five guys would go off the field and only four subs would replace them. The fifth guy would pretend to go off, but he'd stay in bounds, even with the line of scrimmage. When the ball was snapped, he'd take off down the field all alone and our quarterback would throw him the ball. Finn would tell the officials about the play before we'd use it so they'd be aware of what was going on. Clever, huh? If my memory is right, we got one touchdown on that play one year, and just missed another one because the quarterback overthrew the ball.

Before World War II, football betting was pretty much limited to a few important college games that got people excited and promised to be fairly close, like Notre Dame versus Southern Cal, Army-Navy, or Harvard-Yale. People would bet on the team they thought would win, straight up. There was some betting at odds, like in baseball today, but in most games there was such a clear favorite that the books were afraid to take action on them. Then point-spread betting came along and changed everything.

A lot of guys—including my pal Jimmy "The Greek" Snyder—claim to have started the point spread, but I did some research a couple of years ago, and as best I could find out, the guy who really got it going was a Minneapolis gambler and bookmaker named Billy Hecht. He started it in 1946 or 1947. Minneapolis was the national betting center then. Leo Hirschfield's *Green Sheet,* the first national football-betting publication, got started in Minneapolis about that time. Hecht was part of the *Green Sheet* bunch for a while.

Point-spread betting and football went together like peanut butter and jelly. No matter how uneven a game seemed, you could make an interesting betting proposition out of it by giving points to the underdog. Point-spread betting also made football a whole lot more exciting to watch for people on both sides of the action. If you're at a game, and your team is losing by 16 or 17 points in the fourth quarter, you're likely to go home if you haven't bet. But if you took 10 points on the game, you'll cheer your lungs out for that last touchdown, and the guy across from you, who gave the 10, will be cheering just as hard for his team to stop yours. The men who run football like to downgrade the betting aspect of the sport, but I think that if it wasn't for betting football wouldn't be nearly as popular as it is today—or as lucrative for those who play and operate it. The wonder is that nobody thought of point-spread betting sooner.

Other things help make football a great spectator and betting sport. One is that it's such a terrific show. There's the violence part of it that some people like, and the spectacle part that appeals to others. With the cheerleaders and the bands and the big halftime shows, every game is like a holiday. I still get choked up every time I hear great college fight songs like "On, Wisconsin" or that one about the "victors valiant" that Michigan has.

Baseball is called the national pastime, but it's only really popular on the professional, big-league level. By contrast, people all over the country get caught up in football, especially the college variety. It's no accident that college football is strongest in states like Alabama, Nebraska, Oklahoma, and Arkansas, where there's no pro-sports competition to speak of for fan loyalty and news-media coverage. If you live in Lincoln, Nebraska, and don't know your football, nobody'll talk to you.

I think television is what makes football the great betting sport it is, though. Every NFL game is televised, and there are national TV games on Sundays and Monday nights on top of the Sunday regional pro action. In the last several years, since the National Collegiate Athletic Association (NCAA) television monopoly was knocked out in court, there are a half-dozen college games on everybody's tubes on Saturdays as well.

All that TV means that people everywhere are knowledgeable about a lot of teams. No matter where you live, you can have a good line on all the NFL clubs and a lot of college ones, too, from watching them on television. That's different from baseball, where most people only really follow their local teams. Everyone's an expert on football, and you know what experts do when they disagree, don't you? They bet.

THE COLLEGES AND THE PROS

Now, football is football, but for betting purposes the college and professional versions of the game are very different. In fact, it's almost like handicapping different sports.

The biggest difference is in the relative abilities of the teams. In the colleges, a handful of teams dominate, a large bunch is mediocre, and another fairly large bunch is just plain bad. A bad team will almost never beat a top team and will only rarely beat a middle-level one. The middle teams almost always get stomped by the major powers. There's been somewhat more equality among college teams since the NCAA passed a rule limiting schools to a total of 95 football scholarships a few years ago, but the rule hasn't come close to smoothing things out entirely.

The pros, on the other hand, have something approaching parity. I'm not saying that all 28 National Football League teams are equal. I am saying that, on any Sunday, any NFL team has the capacity to beat any other team. That "any given Sunday" line is a well-worn cliché, but it's true nonetheless. Year in and year out, underdogs will win between 35 and 40 percent of all games in the NFL *straight up.* In the vast majority of NFL games, the point spread between favorite and underdog will be 7 points or less. When you pick an underdog in the pros, more often than not you'll really be picking that team to *win the game.* That's not true in the colleges, where the spreads are wider and the betting underdogs are less likely to win on the field.

Professional teams are more equal than college teams because there are fewer of them (28 pro teams to 105 NCAA Division 1-A schools), they have smaller squads (45 players to 70 or 80), and their players are better and more experienced. Also, the NFL has an annual draft in which teams get to pick from among the best players coming out of college in the reverse order that they finished in the standings the season before. In the colleges, it works just the other way: the best teams have all the advantages in signing the best high school prospects. College football is one field in which the old saying "Nothing succeeds like success" really holds.

The way that the college game is played magnifies the gaps in ability between the teams. The colleges permit only 25 seconds between plays to the pros' 30 seconds, and the colleges stop their game clocks after first downs while the pros don't. Those things mean that there usually are more plays in college games and, thus, more chances for the good teams to score.

The larger squads in the colleges also work to the advantage of the better teams. When a good team gets ahead of a poor one by two or three touchdowns, it may substitute for its better players, but, chances are, so will the team that's losing. The top team's reserves are almost always better than the poor team's reserves, and they are trying to impress their coaches by playing well instead of just holding the ball and falling down. Before you know it, the good team is beating the bad team by 30 or 40 points.

Every time a college team runs up a big score, its coach has to take some heat for being a bully. The fact is, the way college football is set up—with its emphasis on the national rating polls and invitations to postseason bowl games—it pays for good teams to try to make an impression by massacring bad ones. That's just the opposite of what happens in the pros. Pro teams play each other year after year, and one that embarrasses a beaten foe by pouring on the points can expect to have a very angry customer on its hands the next time they meet, maybe even later that same season. It's interesting that the pro teams are nicer to their opponents than the colleges, which aren't supposed to be in the football business. But that's the way it works.

It's also a fact that, whatever they may say, college coaches are aware of the point spreads and know that their schools' alumni—who have a big hand in hiring and firing them and keeping their rosters stocked with blue-chip players—appreciate cashing an occasional wager on the old alma mater. The perennial-powerhouse teams routinely go into games favored by 14 points or more, but they still manage to cover the point spread a good percentage of the time. The *Gold Sheet* in 1985 took a look at coaches' lifetime records against the spreads, and the top of the list included Bo Schembechler of Michigan (.589 over 22 seasons), Bobby Bowden of Florida State (.588 for 19), Don James of Washington (.586 for 14), and Barry Switzer of Oklahoma (.577 for 12). Not too shabby, to say the least.

One college team that had a special reputation for beating big spreads was Notre Dame in the late 1960s and early 1970s under coach Ara Parseghian. In those days,

Notre Dame played only two games a year that were predictably tough, against Purdue and Southern California. The rest of the time they played teams like Northwestern, Navy, and Georgia Tech, which they figured to beat handily.

A bunch of guys from the Midwest who followed Notre Dame closely made a bundle betting on the Irish against those "soft" teams during the Ara era. It got to the point where the Las Vegas bookies would sit around trembling, waiting for the "Notre Dame Order" to come in. It didn't come on every Notre Dame game, which kept the books from raising their spreads to the point where it might discourage the normal, very large pro-Irish crowd. But when the Order did come, it was right a high percentage of the time. And when it was wrong, it wasn't for any lack of trying by the team.

One game sticks in my mind. It was in 1969 when Parseghian's Notre Dame team played Georgia Tech in a televised night game. I think the Irish opened as an 18-point favorite, but closed at 23 or 24 points because of a huge Notre Dame Order. Notre Dame dominated the game, and was winning by 18 points in the closing seconds with the ball in Georgia Tech territory. Instead of running out the clock, the Irish called a time-out, then came back with a last-play try for a touchdown pass that failed. After the game, Parseghian was asked why he passed for a score when he was so far ahead. He said something about the pass being to a secondary receiver. Ha! The TV replay showed that his quarterback went to that receiver because the other guy was covered.

PRESEASON NFL GAMES

Another major difference between the colleges and the pros is that the pros play a schedule of four preseason games that aren't reflected in the standings. The colleges have no equivalent of that. Some bettors shy away from betting during the NFL preseason, reasoning that it's tough enough picking winners when the teams are going all out to win the games that count. My view couldn't be more different: *I think that the NFL preseason can be the best time to bet.*

There are basically two ways that NFL clubs approach the preseason schedule. Some—usually the better ones—use it chiefly to evaluate their marginal personnel, especially their newcomers, and try out new play ideas that they would rather not risk when the standings are on the line. Other teams—usually ones coming off bad years—want to get some wins under their belts to put their players in a positive frame of mind for the regular campaign ahead.

It's not hard to tell which teams fit into which categories—you only have to read the newspapers. Most coaches will tell the reporters covering their teams what they plan to do in each preseason contest. During the regular season, the bettor often has to read between the lines to discern a team's intentions in the weekend ahead. During the preseason, he just has to read what's on the lines.

Some beautiful examples came up during the 1985 preseason. In the first weekend of play, the Seattle Seahawks, a playoff team under coach Chuck Knox for two years running, were to meet the Indianapolis Colts, a longtime loser. Seattle's best running back, Curt Warner, had had knee surgery in the off-season, and Knox said in advance that Warner wouldn't play. Otherwise, Knox said he'd be giving his rookies and fringe players a long look.

Indianapolis had a new coach, Rod Dowhower. He wasn't familiar with his first-line players, and he said he planned to give them quite a bit of playing time. You also could be sure that the Colt players would be knocking themselves out trying to look good for their new coach. Seattle went in favored on the basis of their better previous season's record, but the Colts won the game, straight up. So did I.

I employed the same procedure in going 4–0 on Chicago Bears' games in the 1985 preseason. Here was a team that made it to the National Football Conference final the year before with a so-so offense and a great defense. The keys to their offense were quarterback Jim McMahon, who had injured a kidney and missed the last six games of the 1984 regular season, and Walter Payton, the NFL's all-time career rushing leader.

The Bears' first two preseason games were with the St. Louis Cardinals, a good team, and the above-mentioned Colts. Bears' coach Mike Ditka said before each game that he'd play McMahon for one quarter and Payton for maybe one or two series of downs. How did the Bears do? They lost both games, of course, and they didn't cover. Two wins for me, though; I bet against them.

The Bears' next game was with the Cowboys at Dallas, and Ditka, a former Cowboy assistant coach, told the press it was time to stop fooling around. He said he'd let McMahon and Payton each play about a half, and I knew that with the great Bears defense there was no way Dallas would score much. Dallas, which rarely goes all out in the preseason, was a 4-point favorite. A field goal in the final minute gave the Cowboys a 15–13 win, but I had the Bears, so I won, too.

The Bears' last preseason foe was Buffalo, which looked like one of the worst teams in the NFL. Now Ditka says he is going for a win to set up his team for the season. The year before the Bears had pasted Buffalo, 38–9, in their preseason finale. In 1985 they did it again, 45–10. For me, winning that game was like shooting a deer at the zoo, although I'm not a hunter and wouldn't shoot anything anywhere. All it took was reading the newspapers.

GETTING A NUMBER

NFL preseason games aside, a bettor has to have a number to beat a number. By that I mean that you should find a way to quantify for yourself the differences between football teams so that you'll have a firm reason for betting into, or passing, the point-spread lines you'll see during the season.

Some amateur bettors—maybe even most of them—get by strictly on intuition. A few even manage to do pretty well that way. They'll make their own point-spread line by deciding on their "sticking point" between two teams. Say that the Dallas Cowboys are playing the New York Giants at Dallas. They'll close their eyes and concentrate, and decide that Dallas is exactly 4 points better than the Giants. If the line is 3 points or less on Dallas, they'll take the Cowboys; if the Cowboys are favored by 5 points or more, they'll take the Giants. If it hits the 4, they'll pass.

That's okay if you're betting $10 or $20, but bigger money deserves more effort. That's where the subject of power ratings comes in. A power rating gives you a measuring stick that takes much of the guesswork out of picking games. The fact that so many bettors are out there guessing—along with the vig—is the bookmaker's chief ally. His anchor is his number. It's the same reason why a blackjack dealer with, maybe, a high school education is favored at the table over a guy with a Ph.D. The dealer draws on 16 and holds on 17. Period. The Ph.D. guesses. And usually loses.

Now, you can get very, very complicated in putting together a power rating, especially in this computer age. Different guys throw in all sorts of scoring, yardage, and first-down and turnover stuff, and sometimes come up with numbers that have two or three digits *after* the decimal point. I'm no great Figure Filbert, and this isn't a book on higher mathematics. Still, you ought to have a number, and I want to help you get one.

I think that the best way to start is to take advantage of some smart people's work and use a published rating as your takeoff point. Do it during the summer before a new football season, using a final rating list from the year before. I guess that about the most widely published power rating is the *Dunkel Report* that a lot of general-circulation newspapers carry. Mort Olshan's *Gold Sheet* also has a good one, as does the *Sports Reporter.* Mike Lee's service, which operates out of Las Vegas, does a good job on the college numbers. So does *Peach Pix,* based in Augusta, Georgia. I'm sure there are others.

A power rating establishes the point differences between teams that are *100 percent healthy and are playing on a neutral field.* To give you an idea what one looks like, here are the *Gold Sheet's* final NFL numbers for the 1984 season:

San Francisco	−1	N.Y. Giants	11
Miami	0	San Diego	11
L.A. Raiders	4	Tampa Bay	12
Washington	5	New England	13
Seattle	5	Cleveland	13
Denver	6	N.Y. Jets	16
Dallas	7	New Orleans	16
Green Bay	8	Philadelphia	16
Pittsburgh	8	Detroit	17
St. Louis	8	Houston	17
Chicago	9	Indianapolis	20
L.A. Rams	9	Atlanta	21
Kansas City	10	Buffalo	21
Cincinnati	10	Minnesota	23

The lower the number, the stronger the team. Thus, if a healthy San Francisco 49ers met a healthy Green Bay Packers on a neutral field at the end of 1984, the *Gold Sheet* thought the 49ers should have been a 9-point favorite.

From that point, you can go off on your own, revising the numbers as new information comes along. The time to begin this is *before* a new season. The first place to look is at the teams' front offices.

ORGANIZATION

Of all the major sports, football has the most season-to-season continuity. That's because it's the most complicated game, played by the largest squads. It's also because it's the one in which coaching and organization count for the most.

The first rule of football—professional or college—is that *good teams tend to stay good, and bad teams tend to stay bad.* It all starts from the top. Good teams have management and coaching stability and a clear organizational philosophy. Bad teams usually have neither.

For my money, the best-managed professional football teams in recent seasons have been the Los Angeles Raiders, Miami Dolphins, Dallas Cowboys, and Pittsburgh Steelers. Sure, they've had off years, but far more good ones. Their good moves always outnumber their bad ones by many times.

Al Davis owns the Raiders and the Rooney family owns the Steelers from way back. Unlike some NFL owners, football is their main business, so they can give it their full-time, year-round attention. I think that Davis is the sharpest team owner in professional sports. He's a former player and coach, and knows his game from the bottom up. He's a brilliant guy who doesn't buy the conventional wisdom. His teams had a .714 winning mark between 1963 and 1984—the NFL's best—and he's about to collect a huge chunk of money from his fellow owners as a result of all those lawsuits over his team's move to Los Angeles from Oakland. He's eating the other owners' lunches on the field and off.

The Dolphins and Cowboys are owned by people with non-football backgrounds, but they've had the good sense to turn their teams over to savvy football men. Don Shula runs the Dolphins and vice president Gil Brandt and coach Tom Landry run the Cowboys. Their records speak for themselves.

I think Shula is the smartest NFL coach because he has been the most flexible over the years. In the early 1970s, when defense was king in the NFL, Shula had a great one in the "No-Names," and ground out yards on offense with fullback Larry Csonka's runs and quarterback Bob Griese's short passes. In 1979, the NFL changed its rules to let offensive linemen use their hands in pass blocking and prohibit defensive players from bumping pass receivers more than 5 yards past the line of scrimmage. Shula found himself some speedy little receivers and went to a long-bomb passing game. By 1984, his passing game was the best in the business.

All four teams have the kind of coaching stability it takes to succeed. Landry has coached the Cowboys for 26 years; he's the only coach they've ever had. Shula has coached at Miami for 16 seasons and Chuck Noll at Pittsburgh for 13. Tom Flores has been head coach of the Raiders only since 1979, but he was an assistant coach and a player for the team before that.

As for philosophy, there's no one way to build a winner. The Cowboys do it with computers, multiple-set offenses, and clean-cut-type players. Al Davis goes for rough, tough older players, some of whom look like they belong in a motorcycle gang. The important thing is that these teams aren't pulling themselves up by the roots every couple of years. With the top organizations, the players always know what to expect, and what is expected of them.

It works the same way in the colleges. If you think that football is any less of a business there than in the pros, you haven't been paying attention. Schembechler has been grinding out wins at Michigan in front of 100,000-plus home crowds for 23 seasons now and Joe Paterno is still going strong at Penn State after 20 years. Tom Osborne's Nebraska backs have been running the ball behind their huge linemen since 1973, just the way they did for Osborne's boss, Bob Devaney, before that. The good ones go on and on. I think that coaching stability is probably even more important in the colleges than in the pros because of the recruiting side of the college game.

Those points lead into my second football-organization rule: *in the short run, a change in a head coach will make a good team worse, and it won't improve a mediocre or bad one.* There have been all kinds of examples of this. Ray Perkins may turn out to be a great coach at Alabama, but he had a couple of rough seasons after replacing Bear Bryant. The same went for Ted Tollner at Southern Cal when he replaced John Robinson. Look what happened to the Minnesota Vikings the year Les Steckel replaced Bud Grant! I read that the Vikings' management had to about double Grant's salary to get him back for the 1985 season.

Notice that my coaching-change rule is for the short run only. Coaches *do* turn programs around, but it usually takes a year or longer. Mike White made Illinois a winner after a long drought, but he was a loser his first year. Jim Young got Army back on the winning track with the wishbone offense in 1984, but he was 2–9 in his first season at West Point while he was getting acquainted with his players. The list goes on.

My practice on coaching changes is this: I add 2 points to the preseason power rating of a good team with a new head coach, and leave alone the ratings of not-so-good teams after coaching changes.

RECRUITING AND THE DRAFT

The other consideration in evaluating teams before a season starts is the new personnel they take on. NFL teams get their new people through the college-player draft and by signing free agents. Colleges do it by recruiting from high schools. College rosters turn over at a rate of about 30 percent a year, pro rosters at about 10 or 15 percent.

My view on the impact of new players is different from that of a lot of guys: I don't think they have much impact. I know that the NFL draft is very exciting, and that the fans get all worked up over the great draft choices their teams make every year. The truth is that football isn't like basketball, where one new man can make a big difference right away, and not all draft choices even turn out to be players.

The same goes for the colleges. Schools can give out 30 football scholarships a year, but after all the recruiting hoopla is over, darned few of those kids will play much as freshmen and fewer still will start or star. In fact, the trend among the colleges now is to "red-shirt" their freshmen—that is, hold them out of competition for a year—to give them time to mature, grow bigger muscles, and get used to college and their coach's system. I think that's great. I never liked the idea of throwing freshmen right into the college game, sometimes even before their classes start.

Some kinds of players can help a team right away more than others. Defensive linemen and running backs can make the greatest immediate impact. Those are instinct positions that don't require a lot of coordination with other players. A really fast pass receiver sometimes will make a big splash quickly, although even the speediest receiver has to learn some pass routes.

Positions that take longest to fill are quarterback, offensive line, defensive backfield, and linebackers. A new quarterback has a lot of plays to learn, and at every jump (high school to college; college to pro) offensive systems get more complex. Offensive lines, defensive secondaries, and linebackers work as units, so a new man has to fit himself into a scheme.

The NFL draft is supposed to help the weak teams get stronger, and in the long run it can. But I think that the good teams are the most likely to get immediate help from it. Take two recent rookie sensations: Eric Dickerson of the Los Angeles Rams and Dan Marino of the Miami Dolphins. I think that it was possible for Dickerson to step right in and start setting ball-carrying records because the Rams had that great offensive line of theirs ready to block for him. If he'd been drafted by Buffalo or New Orleans, he'd have taken his lumps. Same with Marino. A team like Miami, with an established system and a good overall cast, could work in one or two new guys a year—even a new quarterback—a whole lot easier than teams that are just about starting from scratch. People say that Marino took the Dolphins to the 1985 Super Bowl. I say that the Dolphins took Marino.

I don't make any preseason adjustments to my power ratings based on a team's draft or recruiting crop. I'll watch them play a few games to see if any of the new guys are making an impact.

HOME-FIELD ADVANTAGE

One thing that I certainly do allow for is home-field advantage. I think this is one of the most important—and least understood—aspects of football betting.

Most gamblers, including some professionals, automatically give 3 points to the home team. As a rule of thumb, a 3-point award isn't too bad. As a guide to a bettor who really wants to win, it leaves a lot to be desired.

I don't think the home-field advantage is as strong as it used to be, especially in the colleges. Some years back, college teams rarely left their home areas for games, and the officiating wasn't as competent as it is now. The University of Miami, where I went to school, was pretty isolated from other major football schools. Colleges then didn't like to pay a lot to import officials, so Miami used the same fellows, over and over, for their home games. Needless to say, the officials knew what side their bread was buttered on, and they'd give Miami an edge. The home-field edge there was worth 6 points.

You don't see that today. When a major college team takes a nonconference date, it usually makes sure that at least some of the officials will be from its home region. Sometimes it will bring *all* the officials along. When Illinois and Southern Cal began a home-and-field series in 1985 at

Illinois, all the officials were from the PAC-10. When Illinois was to visit Los Angeles for the rematch, it was supposed to be with all Big 10 officials.

The football pros always have been mature guys who are used to traveling and playing before large crowds. Pro teams now leave for road games a day or two in advance to get acclimated to the new city and make their players comfortable in their hotels. College kids are getting to be more like pros when it comes to travel; they're more sophisticated than they once were. Playing on the road isn't the shock (or thrill) that it was for college players in the old days.

In the pros, I give the home team anywhere from 3 points to none, with 2 points being the average. I give the 3 points to home teams in early season nonconference games. Kansas City, say, might play Washington only every few years, so a trip there might be a bit more unsettling for the Chiefs than one to Denver or Seattle, where they play every year.

As the season goes on, and the games get more important, my home-field edge diminishes. Two points remains my norm, but a team that's going nowhere might get just 1 point in a home game against a club with a playoff berth in sight. For a tail-end team late in a season, I think the home-field edge is nonexistent. How much advantage is there in playing in a stadium where half the seats are empty, or in front of a bunch of spectators wearing bags over their heads?

My home-field edge in college games is a little stronger, running from 2 to 4 points. That's because travel still is more of a novelty to a college kid than to a pro. I give the 4 points to good teams playing at home in nonconference games. Three points is my typical award. Mediocre or poor teams playing conference games at home against a stronger rival get just 2 points unless it's an alumni homecoming game or there's another sort of unusual deal going that might get the home players pumped up.

When it was new, "Monday Night Football" was the NFL's version of a college homecoming game, with home teams beating the spread a high proportion of the time. Being on national television in prime time was a real upper for the home fans, and they'd get into the Monday games more than they would on a typical Sunday. Also, the players would put out more effort because they felt that the other players around the league were at home watching. As the years went by, though, the novelty of Monday night games wore off. They're nothing special now. I used to give an extra point to home teams on Monday night, but I stopped doing that a half-dozen years ago.

Two additional factors tied to the home-field advantage are turf and weather. I don't make special allowances for either.

Conventional wisdom has it that speedy teams have an edge on artificial turf, while ones with grind-it-out offenses do better on grass. I think that speed works anywhere, but that there might be some truth to the latter point. Bill Brown of the Minnesota Vikings and Larry Csonka of the Miami Dolphins were big, rugged fullbacks who liked to wear extra-long shoe cleats on grass to give them more traction, and it might have given their teams a bit of an ege. The Washington Redskins' John Riggins and George Rogers are the same kind of runners today. Still, it's too thin an issue to make me alter my numbers.

When artificial turf first came out back in the 1960s, teams that had it had a point or two extra edge at home, because their opponents weren't used to it. I don't think that holds anymore. Just about all NFL and major college teams have both grass and artificial-turf practice fields, so they can prepare for whatever surface they'll be using that weekend. There are special shoes for every surface today, and every team has them.

The same goes for the weather. I don't think that a team from a warm-weather city has any special edge when it hosts a team from a cold-weather town late in the year, or vice versa. Most colleges play their nonconference games early in the season, so the weather-change issue rarely arises there. And all the pro teams have players from all parts of the country, so we're not talking about a bunch of Hawaiians playing a bunch of Eskimos. Nobody likes playing in cold weather, no matter where he's from. I think it's an equal disadvantage.

I make an exception to my weather-doesn't-count rule for the New Year's Day college bowl games. I think that teams from the East and Midwest give up more than the usual home-field edge when they play against California or southern teams in the bowls. It's not so much the change of weather that does the visitors in—it's the whole atmosphere of the bowl games.

Here's a bunch of young men spending the Christmas holidays away from home. The weather is great and everybody around them is having a good time. The sponsors of the game want to take them to Disneyland and get them into roast beef-eating contests and such. If a coach takes his players away from all the festivities and makes them stick to football, he's like Scrooge and his players get upset. If he lets them participate in the outside stuff, they can't keep their minds on the game. Meantime, the local team has all the advantages of being at home. The poor coach from up north can't win off the field, and he usually can't win on it, either.

INJURIES

Injuries to players are another thing that should make a bettor reevaluate his power ratings. It's also something that most people overestimate. I make some of my biggest bets on teams that get knocked down in the public mind— and in the point spread—because a supposedly key player is hurt.

The position the fans overestimate most is quarterback. They think that if a team's first-string quarterback gets hurt it might as well not show up for its next game. That's baloney. Almost every NFL and major-college team has two competent quarterbacks, and a few even have a third guy who can step in and do a decent job if he has to.

Let's take a hypothetical NFL team as an example of what I mean. The typical pro team runs 65 plays a game. Of these, 30 are runs, 30 are passes, and 5 are punts. A top pro quarterback completes between 55 and 60 percent of his passes—maybe 17 of 30. Say his replacement drops to just under 50 percent, with 14 of 30 completions. That's 3 fewer completions a game. The average pass completion is for about 13 yards. That's about 40 fewer yards passing with a sub than with a starter.

Now, how much is 40 yards worth? My rule of thumb is that 70 yards equals a touchdown, so 40 yards should equal a field goal—certainly no more. Add 2 or 3 points to the rating of a team that loses its No. 1 quarterback, and watch to see how the No. 2 guy does. If he's like Johnny Unitas, who got his break because George Shaw, the regular Baltimore quarterback, was knocked out of a game with Chicago, you'll have to start *lowering* the team's power rating.

Another position that I think is overrated in the public mind is running back. The good ones get a lot of publicity, but except for a few truly great ones—like the Bears' Walter Payton, the Rams' Eric Dickerson, and Ohio State's Keith Byars in 1985—there usually isn't too great a drop between a team's top runner and its second guy. That's especially true among the major colleges, which can be three or even four deep in competent runners.

I think that bettors should be alert for injuries to players on units that *work together as teams*. By that I mean members of offensive lines and defensive backfields. A good offensive line usually takes a couple of years to develop, and if one guy is lost from a top unit it can show up right away. Not only is the team's blocking weaker, but you'll probably see more offsides penalties, because the injured player's replacement won't be as tuned in to the unit's rhythm as the starter was, and more offensive-holding penalties. An injury to a member of a *good* offensive line is worth a point on its power rating. If two guys on the same good line go down, add 2 points right away and more if it looks like the show may be over for that team.

The same, I think, goes for defensive backfields. With the recent rule in the pros against bumping receivers more than 5 yards past the line of scrimmage, this is a particularly vital area. Injuries to defensive backs are hardest on pro teams like the Raiders, Bears, Falcons, and Jets, which play a lot of man-to-man pass defense. Teams can try more zone defenses to cover up injury-caused weaknesses in their secondaries, but that usually just throws other parts of their defense out of whack.

Another position at which injuries can be harmful is defensive line. The rules changes that have opened up the passing game in the pros have put a tremendous premium on the pass rush as a defensive factor. With receivers allowed to race around untouched, any quarterback who has time to throw will complete a very high percentage of his passes. An injury to a top pass rusher like the Jets' Mark Gastineau, the Bears' Richard Dent, or the Giants' linebacker Lawrence Taylor is worth a point to his team's power rating. Add a half-point for the loss of lesser, but still noteworthy, defensive linemen.

For injuries to players who are merely filling space, of course, make no power-rating adjustments. Just because a guy starts doesn't make him good, and most pro and major-college backup players aren't much worse than the guys they replace. Player absences for other reasons—such as disciplinary suspensions, deaths in the family, or contract holdouts—should be counted as if the player were hurt.

As a rule, injuries count for more among the pros than among the top college teams. The pros have smaller rosters, so they lack the depth at every position that the college powers have. Naturally, the worse a team is to begin with, the less it can afford to lose its better players. As the football season progresses injuries tend to pile up, so that just about all teams—pro or college—are hurting at the end of a campaign. The weight of these injuries falls heaviest on the poor and mediocre college squads that are thin to begin with. Your chances of finding "live" big-spread college underdogs (10 points or more) are better early in the season than toward the end.

WEIGHING STATISTICS

Once a season is under way, you'll want to adjust your power ratings to reflect the results of games that have been played. My suggestion is to keep this simple. Focus mainly on the football statistics that count the most: wins and losses.

Basically, a team's power rating should improve (that is, go *down* numerically) if it defeats or plays well against stronger-rated teams. Its rating should get worse (increase) if it does the opposite.

Let the point spreads be your guide in determining the quality of the opposition a team plays. If a team wins a game in which it is a 21 point or more underdog, you should knock 4 points off its rating and add 4 points to the rating of the favorite. If the underdog wins a game in the point-spread range of 14 to 21 points, make that a plus and minus 3 points. A victory over a 10- to 13-point choice is worth 2 points, and one over a 6- to 9-point favorite is worth 1 point.

The magnitude of the win also should be taken into account, but it is important that you consider not only the final score but the manner in which it was obtained. Ordinarily, you don't alter the power rating of a team that beats another of its own level, but if that win was especially impressive, an adjustment might be in order. I define an impressive win as one that was accomplished by 10 points or more, without the benefit of an unusually large number of turnovers by the opposition, and without the sort of late scores that often go against a team that's playing catch-up.

I know that some people will give me an argument on that turnover point. They claim that a good team will find a way to get the opposition to cough up the football. That may be so, but I don't think you can figure in advance that a game will be won or lost on fumbles or interceptions. To the contrary, if a team loses one week because of a high number of turnovers, it often figures to be a pretty good bet the next week.

The main statistic that I look for after the score is how a team does *on the ground*. This is especially important in the colleges. Early in the schedule, when teams are establishing themselves, I want to know if a team can run the ball and keep its opponents from running. A team that can run the ball can control the clock, and will rarely get blown out. A team that can stop its opponents from running will have lots of chances to score and can be expected to capitalize on some of them.

Passing yardage, I've found, is the biggest liar in football. Check the stats after games, and you'll see that as often as not the loser had more passing yards than the winner. I look at passing teams the way I look at certain good-looking guys. They've got the appearance, the manners, and maybe even the clothes and the car. They always make a good first impression with the gals. But during the course of a date they'll find a way to foul up and have to settle for a good-night kiss. Then there are guys who aren't so handsome, don't dress so well, and don't know how to order wine in a restaurant. Maybe they're a little rougher. But they still manage to score more than the pretty boys. They're the runners—the kind of teams I like to back. A good passing attack is a necessity in today's pro game, and it can help a poor team cover a big spread against a better one. But football—college and pro—is basically a physical game that's won or lost in the trenches, and that shows up in rushing yardage.

THE INTANGIBLES

I also look for things that don't show up in the stats. One is a team's flexibility. I'll always give an extra edge to a team whose quarterback can run—scramble, actually—as well as pass, especially in the pros. The NFL today is full of those "situation" defenses that are designed to stop the pass—the ones with five, six, or even seven defensive backs. It's tough to throw against them in third-and-long situations. Thus, a team with a quarterback who can pick up some yards on foot when he has to might make me take a chance on it against a team whose quarterback can't, other things being equal. I'm thinking of Joe Montana of the 49ers, Joe Theismann of the Redskins, Jim McMahon of the Bears, Dave Krieg of Seattle, and Tommy Kramer of the Vikings. Come to think of it, that was about the whole list in the 1985 season. I thought that Montana's running ability was the 49ers' key edge over the Dolphins in the 1985 Super Bowl.

Flexibility shows up, too, in the gimmick plays that some teams have. In fact, I think that if you'll recall the great pro teams you'll remember that just about all of them had something unusual to fall back on in a pinch, just like my high school team's old "sleeper play." With the Vince Lombardi–coached Green Bay Packers of the 1960s, it was the Paul Hornung halfback-option pass; the Bears' Walter Payton does that well today. The great Miami Dolphin teams of the early 1970s had the end-around run with Paul Warfield. John Madden's Oakland Raider teams went in a lot for fake field goals. The Washington Redskins' Super Bowl teams had that "flea-flicker" play where Theismann would hand the ball to fullback Riggins who'd flip it back to Theismann for a pass. A team doesn't have to have a gimmick, but it helps.

An absolute necessity in analyzing a week's games is *checking the teams' schedules for the following week.* Every game doesn't count the same in either the pros or the colleges. Nonconference games are less important to teams than ones within their conferences. Games with occasional foes are less important than ones with traditional rivals.

If Alabama, say, is playing Tennessee-Chattanooga one week and Louisiana State the next, which do you think it will put out most for? How about Dallas versus Kansas City one week and Washington the next? The pros are older than the collegians, and probably less susceptible to the rah-rah stuff, but they take their traditional rivalries every bit as seriously. Familiarity breeds hostility in the NFL. Second games in a season between NFL conference foes usually turn out closer than first games, and often have a different won-lost outcome.

A team that's going nowhere will bust a gut to beat a traditional foe, because a victory will salvage some good memories from an otherwise poor season. And when a good team has something extra going for it, watch out! A perfect case in point was the 1985 college "Revenge Bowl" game between Southern Methodist and Texas. SMU was on NCAA probation for recruiting violations, and a lot of SMU people thought Texas had blown the whistle that put SMU there. SMU couldn't go to a bowl game because of the probation, so it made beating Texas its major goal for the year. SMU went in +6 on the spread. It came out plus-30 on the scoreboard, 44–14.

Another good key that I've used over the years—especially in the pros—is what I call the "extraordinary factor." *If a team has an extraordinarily good or bad game one week, look for it to revert to its usual form the following week.* The factor is especially strong if a team has its unusual game on ABC TV's "Monday Night Football," which more people watch than any other game. If a team looks great on Monday night, everybody will be looking to back it the next weekend, and you'll probably get a real bargain on the spread. Just the opposite goes for a team that laid a Monday night egg. Average-guy bettors place so much emphasis on Monday night games that you'll often get bargains for two or three weeks after one of those extraordinary performances.

GOING AGAINST THE FLOW

If you're a novice bettor, I'm sure that all the advice I've shoveled on you so far sounds pretty confusing. With a little practice, though, you'll quickly get the hang of updating your power rating, and you'll probably find factors I didn't mention to throw into yours. It's a process of trial and error that every handicapper goes through. I'm still fiddling with my figures after more than 30 years. It's an art, not a science, and don't let anyone tell you different.

Once I've got my number on a game, my betting rule in college football is simple. *I'll bet on a college game if my number is 3½ points—half a touchdown—or more different from the bookmaker's line.* That's enough of a cushion to give me the edge I seek.

With the pros, it's a bit trickier. Here, *I look for the "key" numbers 3, 4, 6, 7, 10, 14, 17, 20 and 21. Those are the margins by which many pro games are decided.* Those numbers—or any others—don't hold in college football, where 2-point conversions and easier field goals make just about any margin possible.

I'll bet a pro game with a 2-point difference if there's a "key" number between me and a bookie's spread. Say, for instance, that I make the Denver Broncos 4 points better than the New York Jets. If the spread is Denver minus-3, I'll probably give the points because I'll win on my number—4 (a "key")—and tie on 3, another "key." If the spread is Denver minus-5, I'll pass, because 5 is a "dead" number—few games are decided by that margin. If it's Denver minus-6, I'll take the Jets.

Now let's say that I like Denver by 7 points. If the bookie's number is 6 (a "key" number) or less, I'll give the points, but it would take a spread of 10 points or more to persuade me to take the Jets because few games are decided by 8 or 9 points.

The greater the difference between my number and the spread, the more money I'll be willing to bet on a game. But that's a subject for a later chapter on money management. It's enough to say for now that "key" numbers figure very strongly in my approach to pro football.

That's not all, though. I think that the main reason for my success in football is that *I'm not afraid to back underdogs when my numbers and my instincts tell me to.* I bet on about 65 percent underdogs in the pros year in and year out, and almost 60 percent underdogs in the colleges.

You must remember that a bookie's point spread isn't necessarily his or his handicapper's opinion of the *real* difference between two teams. Rather, it's his opinion of which number will divide the money action on the teams equally so he can get his profit from the 11 to 10 vigorish.

The bookies know that most people would rather bet on favorites than underdogs. They'd rather go with the crowd than stand on their own. Thus the point spreads tend to make it harder for people to play favorites. Stated another way, *the bettor who plays favorites often has to pay for his choice by giving more points than he should.* I know this, and I've made it pay off for me over the years. Now you know it, too.

I'll show you how I put my football guidelines into practice in the final chapter of this book, my betting diary for the 1985 NFL season.

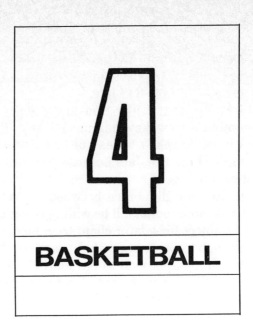

BASKETBALL

Some people say that they don't like basketball. To them, the players are too tall, the basket is too low, and the scores are too high. All you have to watch is the last few minutes of the games, they say. Who cares about a track meet between a bunch of giraffes?

I can only shake my head in dismay over that sort of talk. For my money, basketball is the best played of any of the popular American sports, and the one that has improved the most over the years.

I think the fact that I used to be pretty good at the game myself helps me appreciate basketball more than other people do. Being six feet three inches tall in high school and college, I was always the "big man" on my teams, and I played center. In those days, you could just about bet that any player six feet six inches tall or taller would be a stiff, unable to do anything except maybe put in a layup if nobody was guarding him.

Today, it's amazing what the players can do. A guy who stands six-foot-six probably is a ball-handling guard, and the Los Angeles Lakers' Magic Johnson plays that position at six-foot-nine! Everybody's big, everybody's good, and everybody can shoot. High school kids can dribble with each hand, put the ball behind their backs, and make the kind of double-pump fakes that most pros couldn't do 30 years ago.

There's no big mystery about why this has happened. Reason number one is the postwar opening of college and pro basketball to black athletes. Reason number two is television. It used to be that few kids got to see big-time college games, and the professional game wasn't even around until the late 1940s. Now, there are three or four college or pro games on TV every night in the winter, and all the slow-motion replay stuff they show makes a clinic out of every game.

You get the TV replays in football and baseball, too, but those are different kinds of sports. Baseball is a game of reflexes, and while it might help a kid to watch how George Brett swings a bat, it won't help much unless he's blessed with Brett's eyes and hands. Football is a team game where individual skills take a backseat to coaching innovation in dictating the pace of progress. Unless a kid has got 21 brothers, he can't go out in the backyard and practice his football moves like he can for basketball. I'd bet that a high school all-star team from any big city today could give the old Minneapolis Lakers all that they could handle.

Betting on basketball is also different from betting on football and baseball. To succeed in basketball, you've got to be quick, and you have to have deep pockets. With more than 250 Division I college teams and 23 in the NBA, there are lots and lots of games, and the lines often don't go up until just a few hours before game time. It's not at all like football, where bettors have a week to chew things over before putting their money down.

A lot of money is bet on basketball, but with all the games—as many as 70 or 80 on a typical Saturday during the season—it's spread around more than it is in football or baseball. That means that the bookmakers' lines aren't hammered by betting action the way they are in the other two sports. That's good for someone like me, who keeps his own numbers and is ready to exploit weaknesses in the lines when he sees them. The novice should be careful, though, because basketball attracts a higher proportion of professional action than do the more "public" games of football and baseball. A friend of mine in the brokerage business likes to say that betting on football and baseball is like buying stocks, which a lot of people follow, while betting on basketball is like being in commodities, a more specialized investment. "There are just two kinds of guys in commodities—the quick and the dead," he says. I think he's only partly kidding.

THE COLLEGES AND THE PROS

Basketball is similar to football in that its professional and college varieties don't have much in common from a betting standpoint. In fact, I think that differences between the pro and college games are greater in basketball than in the gridiron sport.

The college game is played over a 40-minute span (two 20-minute halves) with a 45-second shot clock that became standard in the 1985–1986 season. Individual team schedules among major colleges in 1984–1985 ranged from 24 games (Harvard) to 38 (Georgetown).

Season-to-season turnover of first-line personnel in college basketball can run from 0 to 100 percent, but usually amounts to 30 or 40 percent a year. The talent turnover in real terms can be greater, because individuals are more important in basketball than in any other team sport. The loss of a dominant player like Pat Ewing, Wayman Tisdale, Larry Bird, Michael Jordan, or Akeem Olajuwon *has the potential* to sharply change a team's fortunes.

On top of that, you have to realize that in colleges you're dealing with young players who can grow, mature, and improve a lot from one season to the next. And with all the summer camps and leagues they have these days, a lot of them do just that. Even a team with basically the same personnel can change a lot from one season to the next.

There is some continuity in college basketball. Schools like North Carolina, Kentucky, Houston, Indiana, and Notre Dame almost always have good teams, and a lot of others usually are no more than a half-step behind from year to year. But since UCLA won those 10 NCAA championships in the 12 seasons from 1964 through 1975, no team has repeated as national champion and only Indiana has won the title more than once (in 1976 and 1981). Also, we're talking about betting here, and even a small change in a team's overall strength can make a big difference in its success against the spreads.

The situation in the National Basketball Association is altogether different. Professional basketball has had more continuity at the top than any of the Big Three team sports in recent years. In the six seasons from 1980 through 1985, only four teams—Los Angeles, Boston, Philadelphia, and Houston—have appeared in an NBA championship-final series. Los Angeles has won three titles in that span, Boston has won two, and Philly one. I'm writing this chapter in the middle of the 1985–1986 season, and from here it looks like it will be the Lakers and Celtics in the finals again.

As everybody knows, the key to success in the NBA is having a dominant center. All the top teams have them, and the big guys don't graduate or play out their eligibility like they do in college. The rest of the teams have to be bad enough to pick first in the draft in a year when a top center is coming out of college, or smart enough to get one in trade. I think it's interesting to note that two of the three best centers in the pro game today—the Lakers' Kareem Abdul-Jabbar and Boston's Robert Parish—came to their present teams in trade, and the third—Philadelphia's Moses Malone—got to his as a free agent. It makes you wonder about the sanity of the people who let them get away.

More important from a betting standpoint is that the pros play a long, long regular-season schedule of 82 games, plus a playoff schedule that every year seems to get longer and include more teams. An NBA game lasts 48 minutes (four 12-minute quarters) and has a 24-second shot clock. The quick clock means that the players have to hustle up the floor to get their shots off.

Travel is tougher in professional basketball than in any other sport. Big league baseball has a 162-game regular season, but the baseball players play two- to four-game sets in each city on the road, so at least they get to unpack. In the NBA, it's one game in a town and out, battling crazy airline schedules in the worst weather of the year. It's big fellows crammed into tiny airline seats and beds built for average people. It's long games at high speeds against top opposition. Under those circumstances, it's difficult for players to do their best every night, which makes it a tough betting proposition for gamblers.

The bottom line is that I bet the college and pro games very differently. College basketball, with its short schedules, limited travel, and eager young players, *is a very formful game.* I've never had a losing season in college basketball, even though I wouldn't know the players on some of the teams I bet on from the parking-lot attendants at Caesars Palace.

I've bet on NBA basketball in various ways over the

years, and for three seasons before the present one (1985–1986) I didn't bet it at all. I was turned off by the drug scandals in the sport and the difficulty of finding a pattern to the point-spread ups and downs that affect even the best of the pro teams. I keep power ratings on the NBA, but the teams are like the new cars on a dealer's lot—every salesman knows their prices without having to look them up. This season I've been betting the pros mainly on *scheduling and psychology* and doing very well. I can't claim to have figured out the NBA on the basis of a half-season's play, but I think I'm on the right track.

Because of the differences between the ways I play the college and pro games, I'll analyze them for you one at a time, starting with the colleges.

THE COLLEGES: GETTING A NUMBER

The best way to start a first-season betting campaign in college basketball is the same as in football: find a reliable, published power rating and use its closing numbers from the previous season. I can recommend three of the same services I recommended for their football lines: the *Gold Sheet,* the *Sports Reporter,* and Bill Lee's *Peach Baskets* out of Augusta, Georgia. The *Sports Reporter* in particular is good because it follows a lot of small-college teams that don't get much attention elsewhere. I'm not familiar with all the sheets, of course, so feel free to pick another if their ratings have been recommended by someone you respect.

Basketball power ratings work the same way as football ratings do. The better teams get the lower numbers and the weaker teams get the higher ones. At the beginning of February 1986, for instance, the *Gold Sheet* gave North Carolina its best rating among the colleges, a minus-1, followed by Georgia Tech and Duke at 1 (Mort Olshan likes the Atlantic Coast Conference this year). Georgetown, Kansas, Memphis State, and Michigan each got 4 and Louisville rated a 5. The upper end included Manhattan at 41, Dartmouth at 33, and Harvard and William & Mary at 32. Most of the teams got numbers in the teens and low twenties.

Like in football, power ratings are meant to quantify the differences between teams that are 100 percent healthy and playing on a neutral court. If North Carolina were to play Louisville under those circumstances, it would rate a 6-point edge with the *Gold Sheet*'s numbers.

Once again, though, getting a rating is just the starting point. It's how you adjust yours that counts. Here's how I deal with some of the factors you must consider.

THE COLLEGES: PRESEASON ANALYSIS
(GRADUATION LOSSES, RECRUITING AND COACHING CHANGES)

I do one thing in college basketball that I don't do in college football: add to a team's initial power rating when it loses an outstanding player to graduation. That's my recognition of the fact that basketball is much more of an individual sport than football.

Notice, however, that I said an *outstanding* player. I'm talking All-American here, not just any starter. There are so many good young basketball players around these days that almost anyone can be replaced by another kid who'll be just as good once he gets a few games under his belt.

I thought that the loss to graduation of Pat Ewing made Georgetown 4 points worse than they were when they ended the 1984–1985 season. That's the most I've added to a team's rating in a good many years for that reason. In Ewing, we're talking about one of the best rebounders and defensive players in the history of the college game. Guys like that don't come around often.

I docked Oklahoma 3 points when power forward Wayman Tisdale went pro. I penalized St. John's 2 points for the loss of Chris Mullen, its great-shooting guard. Uwe Blab, the seven foot tall center, was worth 2 points to Indiana, and forward Detlef Shrempf was worth the same to Washington. I figured that a few other players, like Villanova's Ed Pinckney and Memphis State's Keith Lee, were worth 1 point. And that was it.

I make no allowances for a team's recruiting. Every player recruited by a major college was all-state or all-something in high school, and most of them turn out to be only ordinary college players. I don't pretend to be able to pick out the few who will be stars before they play their first college games.

My rules on college basketball coaching changes are about the same as those I use in football: *I believe that, in the short run, a change in a head coach will make a good team worse, and it won't help a mediocre or bad team get better.* By a good team, I mean one that ended the previous season with a power rating of 10 or less in a reputable sheet. I dock a good team 2 points when a new head coach comes on board, and watch it closely early in the season to see how it reacts to the new man.

In fact—and this is very important—*I do almost no betting on college basketball for the first month of the season.* I watch the games, read the box scores, and grade the results, but I only rarely bet. That's partly because I'm pretty much tied up with football until after the New Year's Day bowl games. But I also like to think that I could hold off from betting on college basketball until the teams had played for a month even if the football season ended around December 1, when basketball starts.

Waiting a month answers most of my questions about the preseason factors of graduation losses and recruiting and coaching changes, *without costing me a dime.* Why guess about those things if you can wait and see what they'll mean? If nothing less, the wait is an exercise in discipline. I believe firmly that it's one of the main reasons for my success in college basketball over the years.

THE COLLEGES: HOME-COURT ADVANTAGE

The home advantage in basketball isn't the big deal that it is in football and baseball. Basketball is played indoors, so climate isn't a factor. Neither is the playing surface, because they're all pretty much the same. Likewise, no matter where you play, the floor has the same size and markings, and the baskets are in the same places. That's why the standard home-court advantage in college basketball is only 3 or 4 points. That's about the same as it is in football, but proportionately it's less because in basketball games the two teams together usually score about 140 points compared with about 40 points in the gridiron sport.

I think that the home-court advantage in college basketball has diminished as the level of the play has risen and the players have gotten more worldly. Very few kids recruited by major college teams today haven't played in front of big, excited crowds in high school state tournaments or all-star games, and quite a few recruits have gone on the road for those national all-star games that the fast-food companies sponsor. By the time a player gets to college, road trips are old stuff to him.

I also think that a general improvement in officiating has decreased teams' home-court advantages. Yeah, college basketball officiating is far from perfect, and the home team still usually gets the better of the crucial calls. But take it from me, it isn't nearly as bad as it was ten or even five years ago. I remember that the University of Hawaii used to use a couple of refs that visiting teams nicknamed "Frank" and "Jesse," as in James, for the way they robbed them. Just to make doubly sure that that sort of thing doesn't happen to them, I understand that some of the big-draw college independents, like Notre Dame and De-Paul, insist on a say in selecting the officials before they'll accept a date on the road.

Even if the officiating turns out to be less than evenhanded, there's no way that a gambler can know how it will go beforehand. You just have to figure that any official's bias is included in the home team's edge. I don't believe in worrying about things I can't control, and you shouldn't, either.

So what you're really talking about when it comes to home-court advantage is the size and enthusiasm of the crowd. I chart 170 teams, and there's no way I can know what each of their home-court situations is like, but I don't have to know. Teams that are winning draw well and get the home crowd behind them. Teams that are losing don't. Winning teams generally get the 4 points at home from me and losers generally get the 3.

There are exceptions to this. I'll occasionally give 5 points to teams that have exceptional home-court records. Illinois got a 5 from me this season because of a long home winning streak that extended into 1985–1986 and a great record of covering against the spread at its Assembly Hall. Conversely, I gave a couple of the Ivy League teams just a 2-point home-court edge because they drew so poorly. I guess basketball isn't big stuff among the intellectual elite.

I think that the home-court edge varies with the time of year and quality of the opposition. As in football, it's worth most early in the season against nonconference opponents. I'll add a point or two to a team's usual edge under those circumstances, and maybe subtract one for late-season games against conference rivals that are of equal or greater ability.

You also have to be aware that some schools have two "home" courts, and that they're both not worth the same. For instance, St. John's plays home games in its little campus gym in Jamaica, New York, and also at Madison Square Garden. Boston College has the same deal on its campus and at Boston Garden, and Georgia Tech plays some of its important games in the Omni in Atlanta. The "Big Five" Philadelphia schools (Villanova, Temple, La-

Salle, St. Joseph's, and Penn) take some of their home games downtown to the Palestra.

Southern California plays its home games in the city-owned Los Angeles Sports Arena, but gets kicked out every time the circus or other event comes to town. Then it has to play wherever it can. Poor Southern Cal gets only a 1-point home edge from the *Gold Sheet,* and 2 points from me. I usually give the "two-home" teams 4 points at their campus gyms and 3 points downtown.

THE COLLEGES: INJURIES

There are two things you can be sure of when you chart 170 college basketball teams, like I do. One is that many of the teams you follow will have a player or two injured at least slightly at any given time. The other is that you probably won't have heard about it. College basketball doesn't get the national news coverage that baseball and college and professional football do; most newspapers and television stations concentrate on their local teams and those in the top 20 in the wire-service polls. So a lot of the time you'll be flying blind on injuries.

That's not as bad as it sounds, because I think that you can safely disregard most basketball injuries. I'd say that in about 70 percent of all cases a major college team can replace an injured starter or top reserve without suffering. All the coach has to do is look down his bench for another high school all-stater to send in.

More often than not, I find myself betting on teams with routine injury problems against teams that are supposedly healthy. I think that the linemakers tend to overreact to injuries. It's one of my main sources of bargains on basketball.

If a team loses a star—a kid of all-conference ability or greater—the only sensible move for a bettor is to hold off playing it for a couple of games to see how it copes. *In fact, not betting on a game also is the best strategy to follow anytime you're unsure about the injury status of a key player.*

I think that the most damaging thing that can happen to a team is an injury to its top rebounder. Most teams are fairly deep in shooters and ball handlers, but those kids can't do their things unless someone goes up and gets the ball for them. I'll immediately add 3 points to a team's power rating if I learn that its best rebounder is out. I'll add maybe a point or two for a top scorer or ball handler.

Injuries before road games are worse than injuries before home games. The new player the coach puts into the starting lineup at home probably will do well because he's used to the court and the crowd will cheer him on and make him feel good. Chances are greater that he'll screw up under the unfriendly conditions he'll find on the road.

To repeat one thing: when in doubt about an injury situation, pass. There will be enough college action elsewhere to keep you busy.

THE COLLEGES: WEIGHING THE RESULTS

Even though I don't start betting until January 2, I start analyzing games and updating my power ratings right when the season begins. I'm like a professor who has 170 pupils in his class. Every time a team plays, I give it a grade, either lowering (improving) or raising its power rating, or leaving it alone. As with my football ratings, I don't use any complicated mathematical formulas. I evaluate the quality of a team's performance and the quality of its opposition, and make a judgment as to what it's worth.

I'm most impressed when a team wins a game as a road underdog. I'll knock anywhere from 1 to 3 points off its rating when that happens and, usually, add those points to the rating of the favorite it defeats. My rule of thumb is that a road win over a team that's favored by less than 5 points is worth 1 power-rating point, a win over a team favored by 5 to 10 points is worth 2, and a win by a more than 10 point underdog is worth 3.

I'm almost as impressed by teams that beat favorites on neutral courts, like in the tournament at Madison Square Garden in New York that started the present college season, or in the Christmas tournaments that just about every team goes to. My rule of thumb here is that a win over a 7-point favorite on a neutral court is worth 1 power-rating point, a win over a team favored by 7 to 12 points is worth 2, and a win over a 13+-point pick is worth 3.

I'll also alter my power ratings for underdogs who win at home and teams that play tough but lose narrowly against clubs that are rated higher. I don't want to give any firm guidelines here. How many power-rating points—if any—that I'll add or subtract depends on how the games are played. I'm alert for teams that play a string of good games against higher or equally rated foes, particularly early in the season. It's a sure tip-off that veteran players have improved over the summer, or that some new recruits are helping out.

I don't change the power ratings of teams that perform to expectations, whether they win or lose. I'm not impressed by the early-season winning streaks that a lot of teams run up against weaker opposition. I'll wait to see how those teams perform against squads of their own caliber before I decide how good they really are.

By and large, it's whether teams win or lose, and cover the spread, that impresses me, *not the final score of the game.* I think that final scores in basketball are more misleading than in any other sport. Time and again you'll see teams that are ahead by 3 or 4 points with a couple of minutes left go on to win by 10 or 12 points because the other team had to foul to try to get the ball and hurried its own shots in the final minutes. Sometimes even good teams realize that a game is out of reach and get blown out by 20 or more points because they give up at the end.

When a good team loses by an unusually large margin, and I haven't watched the game, I'll make sure to check the box score in the next day's newspaper to see if I can figure out what happened. A lot of times I'll see that it had an off-night shooting, or that the other team got to take all the free throws. I'll take those things into account when I'm adjusting its power rating. *I won't change my power rating of a good team that suffers an upset if I think it's a one-game fluke.*

I watch a lot of college basketball games on television—as many as three at the same time some nights—usually with the sound off. I watch to get a handle on the teams' styles and on how they perform when the going gets tough. Deliberate teams that can hold the score down make good underdogs, and knowing how teams react to pressure can help me decide whether to take them as short-point favorites against teams of similar caliber. I also try to get general impressions that can shed light on whether I have teams rated properly.

I'm as interested as the next fan in the skills of the individual players, but *I don't take man-to-man matchups into account when I do my handicapping.* I leave it to the coach to decide how he'll handle the opposition's seven-foot-tall center when his tallest player stands six-foot-eight. By the time I start betting—8 or 10 games into the season—a team has shown whether it can win in situations like that.

I play college basketball strictly by the numbers. *When my number is 3 points different from a bookmaker's spread after allowing for injuries and the home-court edge, I play.*

I can't overemphasize how much art goes into my college basketball power ratings. I've been keeping them for more than 30 years, and I think I get better at it each year.

Don't think that you can duplicate my better than 60 percent success record in the game your first year out simply by following the general rules I've set down.

I suggest that you spend an entire season keeping and updating your power ratings on college basketball before you start betting serious money. Make mind bets and keep track of them. That way, all you can lose is your mind. (Only kidding.) Wait until you think you've got a good handle on things before you start risking your hard-earned bucks.

THE NBA: PLAYING BY EAR

Just about everything I've said about keeping a college basketball power rating also holds for the pros. The difference is that I don't play the NBA that way. As I said before, I think that the league's long schedule (and the murderous travel that the players have to put up with) distorts form and doesn't lend itself to a by-the-numbers betting approach. With college basketball, I'm the professor grading my class of teams every week. With the NBA, I'm more like a musician who plays music by ear.

I didn't come to this position easily. Before and just after I first came to Las Vegas, professional basketball was one of my strongest games. In the late 1960s, when the NBA was a 12-team league, I did a twice-weekly column and betting line on the pro game for the *New York Post*. At the other extreme, of course, was my abstinence from pro-basketball betting during the three seasons before the 1985–1986 campaign. The ups and downs of the teams, and the drug-taking antics of a few of the more prominent players, were more than I wanted to handle.

One game in particular soured me on the NBA. I took Denver in a game against the San Antonio Spurs at San Antonio a few seasons ago. I'm listening on the radio, and I hear that David Thompson, the Denver star, isn't in the lineup because he's ill in his hotel room. I lost the game, and later I read that Thompson's "illness" was really a drug habit. To me, that was a complete turnoff. There I was, trying to handicap basketball, when it seemed that what I really needed was a course in chemistry.

Another thing that made the NBA a tougher proposition for me was the advent of the 3-point basket. Before the 3-pointer, taking 3- or 4-point underdogs in the NBA was a pretty good bet because teams that were ahead by that much often would give their opponents an uncontested layup in the final seconds and let the clock run out. Now, trailing teams pass up layups to attempt low-percentage shots from outside the 3-point line in the last couple of minutes, and you don't see as many 1- or 2-point games as you used to.

Basically, though, NBA basketball is tough to handicap because of a lack of consistent trends that a handicapper—or, at least, *this* handicapper—can hang his hat on. Below are the won-lost marks and the records against the spread of the 23 NBA teams for the 1984–1985 season. Take a look at them.

	W–L	RECORD VS. SPREAD
Atlanta	34–48	38–43
Boston	63–19	42–33
Chicago	38–44	32–47
Cleveland	36–46	45–36
Dallas	44–38	44–35
Denver	52–30	43–36
Detroit	46–36	41–39
Golden State	22–60	36–41
Houston	48–34	41–40
Indiana	22–60	38–42
L.A. Clippers	31–51	33–45
L.A. Lakers	62–20	38–39
Milwaukee	59–23	50–29
New Jersey	42–40	43–37

	W–L	RECORD VS. SPREAD
New York	24–58	36–43
Philadelphia	58–24	39–40
Phoenix	36–46	31–48
Portland	42–40	39–40
Kansas City	31–51	45–33
San Antonio	41–41	38–42
Seattle	31–51	34–46
Utah	41–41	41–37
Washington	40–42	41–38

Pretty much of a mishmash, huh? The best team against the spread was Milwaukee with 63 percent winners, the worst was Phoenix at 39 percent. That's a very small spread between top and bottom.

Two teams—the L.A. Lakers and Philadelphia—had overwhelmingly winning records on the court but *losing* records against the spread. Twelve teams—Atlanta, Detroit, Golden State, Houston, Indiana, the Lakers, New Jersey, Philly, Portland, San Antonio, Utah, and Washington—were within three games of .500 against the points in the regular season. That's an awful lot when you're talking about an 82-game schedule.

I came back to the NBA in the 1985–1986 season. I liked the fact that the league was trying to do something about drug use by players. Also, reading in the papers how so many baseball and football players had drug problems led me to the sad conclusion that this kind of thing had come to be a regular part of sports. I can't figure out why healthy young athletes jeopardize their big-buck careers to get "high," but I'm not alone in that.

This time, however, I decided to try to take advantage of the ups and downs of the NBA teams instead of fighting them. I stopped looking at games one at a time, and began looking hardest at whom teams played last and whom they were going to play next. I concentrated on figuring out when teams would be ready to play big games and when they'd be taking the breathers that their killer schedules necessitate. The result: so far, so good.

One thing I see again and again is a good team taking it easy on a poor or mediocre foe when its next game is against another good team. Say that Boston is playing mediocre Washington on Tuesday and arch-rival Philadelphia on Wednesday. Which game do you think the Celtics will put out for? Washington or its counterpart, with the points, would be a good bet, at home or away.

Poor or mediocre NBA teams seemingly decide in advance which games they can win on the road, and which they can't. Say that Cleveland has back-to-back road dates against the L.A. Lakers and Golden State. My guess would be that it would rest up against the mighty Lakers, even if it meant taking a pounding, in order to have something left for a "winnable" game against weak Golden State a night or two later.

Special circumstances can inspire a team to play way over its head. On January 13, Walter Davis came out of drug treatment to play his first game for Phoenix in more than a month. The Suns were at home against San Antonio, and a big crowd showed up. Davis made a speech apologizing to the fans and the team. The Suns went out, won big, and covered.

When that happens, I always look for a quick relapse. And sure enough, the Suns got buried by the Lakers in Los Angeles the next night.

An even better example of that came on February 1 and 2 with the Chicago Bulls. On February 1, the Bulls took a 16–31 record into a home game with the tough Houston Rockets, who were 32–14 and leading the Midwest division. Michael Jordan and Orlando Woolridge, the Bulls' two best players, were out with injuries, and the team was a 2½-point underdog at home. The twist was that the game was nationally televised by CBS—the first time the Bulls had been on the national network tube in four years. A noisy crowd turned out Saturday afternoon and the Bulls pounded the Rockets, 132–122.

The next night, the Bulls went on the road to play Indiana, one of the two teams in the league with a worse record than theirs. Do I have to tell you what happened? They got whipped by 25 points. Alert bettors had two good wins.

I think that the *revenge factor* is as big in the NBA as it is in the NFL, and maybe bigger. When a good team has been upset by a bad or mediocre one, I look for it to pour on the points the next time the two teams play.

I also look for different outcomes in close-together games involving teams of nearly equal ability. Say that Dallas and Utah, two very similar teams, have home-and-home games scheduled. The standard home-court advantage in the NBA is 4 points. That's a total swing of 8 points in the spread on either of the teams for home court alone. If Dallas were to lose narrowly in game one, I'd look for it to make a bigger than usual effort to win a rematch soon afterward, and the same for Utah.

When a team is on the road for a large number of games—four or more—I look for weak efforts in the middle games of the trip and a good one in the final game, when home is in sight. I've been surprised to notice that teams returning from long road trips often don't do well in their first game back home. I think it's because their wives or girlfriends dump all their problems on them when they come home, and they're distracted.

It ought to be obvious to you that you can't always find games that fit my NBA criteria and, in fact, I don't play the pros nearly as heavily as I do the colleges. It also ought to be obvious that none of my NBA "keys" is surefire. Still, I had better than 80 percent winners on the league the first two months of the 1985–1986 season, and I've topped 60 percent since. I think I'm on to something.

RESPECT THE LINE

Like I said before, basketball is more of a professional game than either football or baseball when it comes to gambling. The betting lines go up, get played fast, and come off, without the pounding (and distortion) by the public that you see in the other two major sports. You have to make judgments fast, and this takes practice. Don't rush into basketball without at least some preparation.

It's very important in basketball to shop the lines. When you bet games in volume like I do in the college game (I usually play between 60 and 80 games a week), a point here or a half-point there can make the difference between winning and losing financially. I wouldn't recommend betting on college basketball if you have only one betting outlet. At the very least, don't be shy about asking your bookie for a half-point here and there.

WATCH YOUR ROLL

Don't go into basketball betting in a serious way without a big bankroll. There are lots of games, and you can disappear without a trace in no time flat. In chapter 7, on money management, I provide some betting guidelines for basketball.

BASEBALL

Baseball has a long, long season—six and a half months—and it claims more casualties among bettors than any other sport. Facing all those games, over all those weeks, the average gambler is like a man trying to cross the desert after his car breaks down. He's got no map, he's dressed wrong, and he doesn't have enough water. It's no wonder that a lot of players—and even some bookmakers—never make it to the Fourth of July.

One reason that baseball is so tough is that it is bet into a money line rather than the point line of football and basketball, and a lot of fellows who are successful in those last two sports have a tough time making the transition. In football and basketball, you can take an underdog with the points and still win your bet even if your team doesn't win the game. In baseball, an underdog has to win in order for its backers to collect.

Baseball is played to betting lines that range from a 10-cent spread between favorites and underdogs to a 20-cent spread. Let me give you a fast piece of advice: if all you can get is the 20-cent line—or even a 15-cent line—*don't bet!* There's just no way you can beat it day in and day out. Say that you see in your newspaper that San Diego is a 6 to 7 favorite over San Francisco. That means that you'll win $1.20 on a $1.00 bet if you take the underdog Giants, but you must risk losing $1.40 to win $1.00 on the favored Padres. That's a sucker bet if there ever was one, and it's your fault if you take it.

In the places where I bet in Las Vegas, the 10-cent line prevails, and it can give the gambler a better break than the 11 to 10 line that prevails in football and basketball. In a pick 'em game, both sides usually must put up $1.05 to win $1.00, which is half the vig as in the 11 to 10 sports. After that, the line moves up in 10-cent jumps in a way that returns slightly more than a straight 11 to 10 wager.

A table listing baseball payoffs is at the end of this chapter, but one quick example will tell you how the dime line works. Say that the Chicago Cubs are 5½ to 6 over the New York Mets. A $1.00 bet on the underdog Mets will bring the winner $1.10, while the Cubs backer has to risk $1.20 to win $1.00. As you can see, it's still a tough proposition, but not impossible.

The other big thing making baseball tough is that form does not hold in it the way it does in football and college basketball. In those two sports, the best teams can win—and the worst teams can lose—almost all of their games. But in baseball the best teams win roughly 60 percent of the time, while the worst teams win almost 40 percent.

Also, baseball teams tend to run hot and cold over the 162-game regular season, winning four of five here and losing four of five there. If you get caught in one of those down-drafts, a whole season's winnings can be blown away in a week. That's why proper money management is more important in baseball than in any other sport.

There are, however, several factors that make baseball an attractive game to bet if you have the stamina and discipline. One is that good information on the game is easy to come by. There are only 26 major league teams to follow, and just about every big-city daily newspaper carries up-to-date box scores, standings, batting and pitching statistics, game accounts, roster changes, and injury reports on all the teams. So wherever you live, nothing much will happen without your knowing about it.

I think that baseball gives you a more honest game for your buck than the other professional team sports. From the time the season begins the first week of April until September 1, when rosters increase from 25 players to 40 and managers of losing teams start looking to find out what some of their minor-leaguers can do, every team is putting its best foot forward every inning. That also goes for the individual games. In football or basketball, you can lose a bet on a point-spread favorite because it can go into a "prevent" defense or delay offense in the late going when it is safely ahead. But you can be sure that a baseball team that's winning by 3 runs will be shooting for more when it comes to bat in the bottom of the eighth or top of the ninth inning.

Baseball being as tough as it is, a lot of bettors try to work out systems to beat it. I'm an expert on these systems because I've used about all of them at one time or another. Suffice it to say that none of them works well enough to keep a player in the game for very long. If they did, there would be no bookies left to take their action. But all produce some winners for some people some of the time, and shouldn't be overlooked.

The most common—and simplest—system focuses on teams on streaks. Once a team wins or loses three games in a row, you keep betting on or against it until it reverses its form. The advantage of this system is that it permits you to win a lot of bets while losing just once. The disadvantage—and it's a killer—is that the more a team wins, or loses, the bigger favorite or underdog it gets to be, so that you will find yourself laying big spreads to get your team. Losing a bet laying 8 to 5 or 9 to 5 odds is almost like losing two bets, so you'll have to win two to cover the inevitable defeat.

A couple of other systems have to do with progression wagering, which involves increasing the amount of money you bet on consecutive games so that you can come out ahead if you win just one of a group of wagers. The classic baseball progression player takes a three-game series between two teams and makes a bet on the team he thinks is the stronger, whatever the circumstances. If he wins the first time, he quits ahead. If he loses, he increases his next bet on the next game to where it covers his losing first bet. If he loses two, he makes his third bet large enough to cover both losses. The problem here is easy to spot. It takes a big bankroll to embark on this, and if your favorite is swept in a series, you're dead.

I did pretty well for a while with a system that had about the same handicapping premise as progression wagering, but a different money-management system. I'd choose a team I liked in the first game of a three-game set and bet on it, no matter who the pitchers were or where it was played. If I won the first day, I'd bet again the next day, *only a smaller amount,* so that I'd be ahead for the series even if I lost. If I won the second day, I'd quit, way ahead. If I lost the first day, I'd increase my wager the second day. If I lost the second day, I'd bet again on my team the third day, not on a strict progression system, but enough to recoup part of my losses. The theory is that a baseball series is like a three-round fight, and that the better team should win two rounds, or, certainly, one. The problem again, of course, is a three-game wipeout.

One of the flashier—and riskier—systems I've seen around Las Vegas was invented by a guy named Leroy. He was a dishwasher in one of the hotels who was said to have launched his gambling career with $50 he borrowed. He ran it into tens of thousands of dollars before he was shot down, in the meantime becoming something of a legend along the Strip.

This was in the middle 1960s, when a handful of premier pitchers, like Sandy Koufax, Bob Gibson, and Juan Marichal, were really hot. Leroy's system was to back these guys when they pitched and he thought the situation was right, no matter what the price. The bookies made Leroy pay up the nose for his "big" pitchers. They'd open a Koufax game at, say, 2 to 1, and if Leroy started betting they'd make him walk the ladder with each couple of thousand dollars to where he was laying 13 to 5 or even 3 to 1. But Leroy jockeyed his bets well enough to run up a nice bankroll before the inevitable losses brought him back to washing pots and pans.

Most people, of course, bet on baseball by trying to analyze the games one by one, based on the relative merits of the teams involved. This is what most people do in football and basketball, but there's a difference: in the other two sports, the point-spread lines allow you to translate team strengths into scoreboard points, whereas baseball's money line makes you convert them into cash, a more difficult intellectual process.

The common way to bet on baseball is to accept the maxim that pitching is 70 percent or so of the game and really bet on the starting pitchers. That is why so many big-city newspapers carry pitching lines that give the season marks of the day's starters, their history against the team they are facing, and the records of their last three outings.

The typical bettor's first decision will be on the dollar difference between a game's starting pitchers. Let's say the Toronto Blue Jays have Doyle Alexander going on the mound against the Boston Red Sox's Bob Ojeda at Boston. Alexander has seven wins and three losses and an earned run average of 4.07 against Ojeda's four wins and one loss and 2.25 ERA, so the bettor will be arbitrary and make Ojeda, say, 20 cents better on the basis of ERA.

Then he'll run down the eight-man lineups of the two teams, position by position. At first base, he'll make Toronto's Willie Upshaw and Boston's Bill Buckner even. He'll maybe figure that Toronto's Damaso Garcia, an all-star, is a nickel better than Boston's Marty Barrett at second base. At third, he'll rate Boston's Wade Boggs a nickel better than Toronto's Rance Mulliniks, for Boggs' bat. He'll give that elusive nickel back to Toronto for slick Tony Fernandez at shortstop over Glenn Hoffman.

Toronto's Ernie Whitt and Boston's Rich Gedman check out about even as catcher. So do the two outfields of Jim Rice, Dwight Evans, and Tony Armas for the Red Sox and Lloyd Moseby, Jesse Barfield, and George Bell for the Blue Jays. Same for designated hitters Mike Easler of Boston and Jeff Burroughs of the Jays. But give the Jays a nickel edge in the bullpen for their Bill Caudill and Gary Lavelle.

Using the football model of the standard, 3-point home-field edge, he'll give Boston 10 cents for being the home team, the same as everyone else. That would make Boston a 20-cent overall favorite in the game. He'll bet if the line comes up outside that number by a certain amount.

I challenge that system on a number of points. *First,* I think that while pitching is certainly the most important single aspect of baseball *starting pitching shouldn't be the overwhelming factor in handicapping two teams.* First, baseball pitching staffs are as specialized as hospitals these days, with every team having long relievers, "setup" men, and short-relief "stoppers" as well as starters. Starting pitchers rarely finish games, often last no more than five or six innings, and often don't get the win or the loss. It's silly to base your major betting decision primarily on two pitchers who as often as not won't figure in the way the game turns out.

Second, baseball teams don't match up position against position the way basketball teams do, or the way football teams do on an offense versus defense basis. In our hypothetical Boston-Toronto game, the only way first basemen Buckner and Upshaw would meet is if one walked or hit a single, and stopped to chat at the bag. Batters face pitchers—not other batters—and that's the way they should be judged.

Third, baseball parks differ from one another in many more ways than do football stadiums. In football, fields are standard in size, and maybe 75 percent of all professional and major college teams play their home games in front of good-sized crowds that root strongly for them. In baseball, parks are different shapes and sizes and so are the sizes and moods of the crowds that watch teams play. It doesn't make sense to assign a standard value to the home-field advantage in baseball.

HOME-FIELD ADVANTAGE

I take the assessment of the home-field edge in baseball very seriously. For me, it's a general decision on a team's management, its overall strengths and weaknesses, and its "fit" with its ballpark. My scale runs from a 20-cent edge for the best home teams to zero for the worst.

In June of 1985, when this chapter was written, I gave a 20-cent home-field edge to five teams: the Chicago Cubs, Boston Red Sox, Toronto Blue Jays, Detroit Tigers, and New York Yankees. I thought that the neatest "fits" between park and team were provided by the Cubs and Red Sox.

The Cubs had a team that was just about perfectly suited to play in Wrigley Field. The prevailing wind there is out to left field, and in Keith Moreland, Ron Cey, and

Jody Davis the team had three right-handed power hitters who could take full advantage of it. Other teams can hit homers in Wrigley, too, so General Manager Dallas Green went out and got his Cubs some low-ball pitchers who could force the opposition to hit grounders. Steve Trout and Dennis Eckersley were two of the best at that. With the Cubs finally winning after so many bad years, the Wrigley Field crowds were big, noisy, and pro-Cubbie all the way.

The Red Sox weren't too far behind in the "fit" department. They had a host of right-handed hitters who could feast on the short "Green Monster" left-field fence in Fenway Park. The fence gives them the additional edge of hypnotizing visiting hitters into altering their usual batting strokes, almost always to their detriment.

The Red Sox usually are short in the pitching department, but I think that their hitting in Fenway offsets that. In 1984, they batted .305 at home and .269 on the road. At this writing, their pitching seemed improved enough to justify the 20-cent rating. Also, their fans always are among the game's best.

Toronto had the speed to play its artificial-turf field well—especially second baseman Garcia and shortstop Fernandez. They also had hitting power and enthusiastic fans. The Yanks and Tigers rated a 20 in June mainly because of their balance. In Dave Righetti, the Yanks had just the left-handed relief pitcher they needed in their short right-field park, and their fans come to the games with a win-or-else attitude (copied from owner George Steinbrenner) that the team finds tough to ignore. The Tigers had the personnel to play anyone anywhere. In 1984, they were the American League's best home team *and* its best road team.

At the other extreme of my scale were the Pittsburgh Pirates. I gave them no edge at all when they played at home. The team was on the sales block and no one—press, players, or fans—knew who would own them or in what city they would play next. Management was trying to peddle players with big salaries, so the team's roster was in turmoil. Crowds were small and turned hostile when the Pirates fell behind.

Not much better off were the San Francisco Giants, Cleveland Indians, and Milwaukee Brewers. The Indians hated playing in their big, gloomy Municipal Stadium on Lake Erie (I read that first baseman Mike Hargrove said that there wasn't anything wrong with the place that a case of dynamite couldn't cure), and their only edge was that visiting players liked it even less. Pretty much the same thing held for the Giants at cold and windy Candlestick Park, and San Francisco is a lot better place to visit than Cleveland. The Milwaukee Brewers weren't quite as bad off as those two teams, but I think their whole organization took a dive after their 1982 American League pennant, and that their ballpark gave them no special edge.

I gave the rest of the teams 15-cent or 10-cent homefield advantages. In my 15-cent group were St. Louis, San Diego, Houston, Los Angeles, the New York Mets, Baltimore, and the Chicago White Sox. Getting 10 cents were Atlanta, Philadelphia, Montreal, Cincinnati, California, Kansas City, Seattle, Oakland, Texas, and Minnesota.

Needless to say, I change my ratings as I think conditions warrant. For instance, although my view that the Chicago Cubs were a great team for their ballpark didn't change, my ranking of the team certainly did when its starting pitchers began to fall to injuries as the 1985 season wore on. Without pitchers, a team can't win in its own locker room, and when all five of the Cubs' top starters were on the disabled list at the same time in mid-August I dropped the team to a 10-cent home edge from 20 cents.

I promoted the St. Louis Cardinals from my 15-cent group to my 20-centers in July when it became apparent that Whitey Herzog had put together a group of speedsters that could take full advantage of the artificial turf in big Busch Stadium.

RATING THE GAMES

After I've assigned each team a home-field price, I calculate the difference between the day's starting pitchers. My formula works like this: *I compare the earned run averages of the two starters and award 20 cents a run for the difference.*

Say, for example, that the San Diego Padres are playing the San Francisco Giants at San Francisco, and that Dave Dravecky is pitching for the Padres against Bill Laskey for the Giants. Dravecky's ERA is 2.40 to Laskey's 4.19, a difference of 1.79 runs. I multiply that by 20 cents (.20) and get a 36-cent advantage for the Padres.

I get my offensive numbers by comparing the two teams' on-base averages. OBA includes walks and safe-on-errors as well as base hits and, thus, gives a better look at a team's full offensive capability than does a simple batting average. *USA Today* carries on-base averages at least once a week during the baseball season. In my Padres-Giants game, the Padres' OBA was .320 to San Francisco's .272. Subtracting the two gave the Padres another 48 cents in my system.

Then I look not only at the teams' bullpens, but also at *whether their key relievers had worked more than two innings the night before.* I give an edge to teams with "big" relief pitchers like Bruce Sutter of the Cardinals, Willie Hernandez of the Tigers, Goose Gossage of the Padres, and Lee Smith of the Cubs *if* the opposing team doesn't have a reliever who is nearly as good, and *if* the big boys haven't gone hard the night before.

Certain factors *don't* enter into my considerations. One is managing. Baseball isn't like football or basketball, where decisions have to be made quickly while play is in progress. In baseball, things move so slowly that a manager has a chance to consult with his coaches or anyone else he wants to before changing pitchers or putting up a pinch hitter. And with all the computers baseball teams use these days, the choice usually has been made for him. I figure that every big-league manager knows about the same amount of baseball as every other manager, and lots of others, too. I think that Harry Caray probably could do about as good a job of managing the Cubs as Jim Frey.

I also ignore injuries to individual players unless the player is of all-star quality. If an average starter is hurt another big-leaguer will take his place, and he'll usually be about as good as the guy he fills in for. Moreover, the 162-game season forces managers to rest all of their players once in a while, and just about everybody—including the stars—sits out 10 to 15 games a year. Managers usually don't announce in advance their intentions to rest players, so as often as not the team you are betting on won't field its strongest lineup. That's something you have to accept in baseball. If a star is hurt, I'll watch the team play a few games to see how it handles the loss.

(Naturally, I also can't ignore mass injuries, like the ones that hit the Cubs' pitching staff in mid-1985. If two or more key players from a team are certain to be out for a game, I'll knock a nickel or dime off their price. If I'm uncertain about a team's injury situation, I'll pass its game altogether.)

I'm not a big believer in what gamblers call "book plays" in baseball. These are the bets based on information about how certain pitchers perform against certain teams, or in certain ballparks. Many—maybe most—baseball bettors follow this information closely, which is why almost every newspaper pitching chart includes it. I'm just as aware of this material as anyone, *but so are the bookmakers, and it's reflected in their lines.* You can argue with me about this if you like, but it's my observation that most of the stuff you hear about how a certain pitcher loves facing this team but hates facing that one is a temporary fluke that evens out in time in the direction of his usual performance. Exceptions are so few that they merely prove the rule. I'll stick with my own numbers and buck public opinion on this.

I don't apply my formulas blindly. If a starting pitcher has an astronomical earned run average because he hasn't worked much, I'll give him an ERA of 6 runs because I figure that his manager wouldn't use him if he thought he was worse. If he's a new pitcher, just up from the minors, I'll give him an ERA of 5 runs.

A FEW EXAMPLES

Let's try a couple of examples to show how my system works. In that San Diego–San Francisco game I described above, I gave the Padres 36 cents for Dravecky over Laskey, 48 cents for their edge in on-base percentage, and a nickel for their having Gossage in the bullpen because the Giants didn't have a comparable reliever. That gave San Diego a plus-89 cents. The Giants' only advantage was their home-field nickel, so the Pads wound up plus-84 cents in my book, a very big advantage. I usually bet a game if the bookmaker's line is 15 cents different from my number in either direction. Thus, I would have bet on the Padres if they were under 8½ to 5 favorites, or I'd have taken the Giants if they were underdogs by 2 to 1 or more.

Now here's a game matching the Chicago White Sox and the Boston Red Sox at Chicago. Bruce Hurst, with an ERA of 3.88, started for Boston against the White Sox's Rich Dotson, whose ERA was 3.59. That came to a .29-run edge for the White Sox. Multiplied by 20 cents (.20), it gave Chicago a 6-cent edge in pitching.

The Red Sox went into the contest with an on-base percentage of .290 against the White Sox's .269, a difference of 21 cents. The White Sox got 15 cents in my book for being the home team. The two bullpens—really, the White Sox's Bob James against the Red Sox's Bob Stanley—shaped up even. The game worked out dead even. If either team was favored by 15 cents or more, I'd take the under-dog.

In practice, my system usually gives me more under-dogs than favorites, and that's the way I like it. I don't care how good a team you're backing, if you give odds of 7 to 5 or more consistently, you'll wind up the season a loser. To win at baseball, you must—I repeat, must—have a large number of underdogs come through for you.

I'm often asked whether my baseball-betting system is arbitrary. Of course it is, but so is every other system that tries to convert comparisons of the abilities of human beings into dollars and cents or, for that matter, score-board points. The point is, having my own number means that I'm not just out there guessing against the bookmak-ers' lines. It's my map to help guide me through the desert.

My baseball-betting plan doesn't end with my rating system. I'm always on the lookout for additional factors that can give me an edge. I've found two of them that have proved useful over the years.

One is to bet against teams that are just coming home after long road trips, especially if they are favorites and are playing their first home game during the day. The assump-tion is that players love "home sweet home," but I'm not so sure that's always true, especially for the married ones. A player will come home from a trip and his wife will be right there to tell him about her problems with the kids and all the things that need to be fixed around the house. She'll also expect to be entertained that night. That can make for some tired home-team players the next day. (You'll recall that I look for this in NBA basketball, too.)

I've also found that pitchers coming off injuries tend to do poorly in their *second* starts after their return. They may do okay the first time out because they'll be rested, but their inaction will catch up with them the next time. I've won three good-sized bets off that key in the last two weeks alone.

THREE RULES

On top of that—and even more important—I follow some rules that I credit as much as my rating system for the success I've had with baseball in recent seasons. They have to do with the discipline it takes to beat a game that comes at you seven days a week from the beginning of April until the middle of October.

My rule number one is that *I never bet seriously on baseball until after my birthday, which is May 4.* It takes that long for teams to compile the statistical records that my rating system requires, and it simply doesn't pay to rush things. Teams can change a lot from season to season, and if you try to pick winners with the teams' previous year's stats—or on spring training results—you're back in the desert walking around in circles.

Rule number two is to *shop the odds* if I can, because this pays off in baseball more than in any other sport. The fact that there are so many baseball games—and relatively little play on many of them—means that lines on the same game can differ widely at the various Las Vegas betting establishments. Rare is the day that I can't get an extra dime or even 15 cents on games I want to play by shopping and waiting for late line changes. Over the season, this can make the difference between my winning and losing.

Shopping for odds also allows me to make an occasional dollar or two by "scalping," or capitalizing on the differences between the betting lines at different bookmaking shops. Stock market guys tell me that they do the same thing and call it "arbitrage."

The other day, for example, one bookmaking shop had the Pittsburgh Pirates favored over the Philadelphia Phillies by $1.10 to $1.00, and another house had the Pirates a $1.15 to $1.25 favorite. At the first book, I bet on the Pirates, putting up $3,300 to win $3,000. At the other, I took the underdog Phillies, putting up $3,000 to win $3,450. If the Pirates win, my bets cancel out and I break even. If the Phillies come through, I'm up $150. You don't find those deals very often—maybe only two or three times a week around Las Vegas—and the payoffs aren't huge because the books won't take unlimited play on baseball. But what the heck, it pays for dinner.

Rule number three couldn't be simpler: *don't be afraid to pass on games.* I always pass if my number comes within 15 cents of the line, and I'll sometimes do the same if it's greater and there's something about a game I'm not sure of, such as the physical condition of a starting pitcher, key reliever, or hot hitter. Sure, I sometimes miss bets that I might have won, but I think I more than make up for it with the money I save on losses. There are 12 or 13 big-league baseball games almost every day, and I rarely bet on more than 6 of them. The average bettor would do well to hold his action to 3 or 4.

My last point about betting on baseball isn't as much of a rule as a philosophy. Proper money management is something I believe in all the time, and I'll deal with it

BASEBALL LINE ON $1.00 BET

| ODDS | PAYOFFS | |
	ON FAVORITE	ON UNDERDOG
Even	$1.00 (or $1.05)	$1.00 (or $1.05)
5–5½	.91	1.10
5–6	.83	1.20
5–6½	.77	1.30
5–7	.71	1.40
5–7½	.67	1.50
5–8	.62	1.60
5–8½	.59	1.70
5–9	.55	1.80
5–9½	.53	1.90
1–2	.50	2.00
1–3	.33	3.00

more fully in chapter 7. But in no sport is it more important than baseball.

If you bet baseball in any serious way, you'll be sure to hit losing streaks, and if you can't handle them, they'll kill you. The unpleasant fact is that it's darned near impossible to survive the baseball season without an outside source of income. When you're losing, you must cut back your bets, and when you're winning, you'll need the courage to take advantage of it by boosting your action, especially when there are large differences between your numbers and the betting line. I can't give you any formula for this; you'll have to figure it out for yourself. Try hard not to let your education get too expensive.

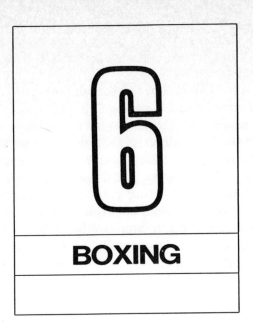

BOXING

I think that if I lived in Denver or Washington or somewhere else where they don't have too many prizefights I would rarely bet on boxing. There aren't that many interesting fights these days, and the sport isn't too good a betting proposition if you're not plugged in to it. But I live in Las Vegas, where maybe 50 percent of all the important championship fights in the United States take place (where else would people pay the outrageous ticket prices that promoters ask?), and once the hype is on I usually get hooked.

I've been a sucker for boxing since my childhood in New Jersey, when I went to the fights with my dad. Boxing was big stuff in the 1930s and 1940s, and the newspapers really played it up. I'd read about a fight for weeks before I'd go to it, and I'd get all excited. I guess I'm still the same way. And if I go to a sporting event, I usually wind up betting something on it.

I go to the fights with two minds. I have nothing but admiration for prizefighters, whom I consider the bravest and best conditioned of athletes. I might criticize a fighter's skill or judgment, but I'll never question his courage. I did a bit of boxing (just a bit) in my younger days, and I know that just stepping into the ring against another man who wants to hurt you takes more guts than just about anything else in sports. Boxing is a way out of poverty for most of the men who take it up, and I'd hate to see that avenue closed to them.

On the other hand, I think there's a lot to be said for banning boxing outright, or, at least, eliminating some of its more brutal aspects. I've seen amateur fights on television, with their headgear and three-round limits, and I like them. I don't know why all boxers shouldn't wear headgear. Three rounds may be too short for bouts between mature men, but six or eight rounds ought to be long enough to decide who's best. Change the rules so you give a fighter as much credit for a stiff jab as for a roundhouse right, like they do in the amateurs. Stop a fight right away if one guy gets wobbly. Use those gloves without thumbs to keep eyes from getting poked. It'd still be boxing as far as I'm concerned. I'm not one of those fellows who has to see blood to be happy.

I have a lot of feeling for boxers because I've known quite a few of them. Las Vegas is a favorite hangout for fighters, especially retired ones. I'm proud to say that I was a friend of Joe Louis in the years that he spent there before he died. If you don't remember the 1940s, you can't appreciate how enormously popular Louis was and how much he meant to many people, white as well as black. My family was Jewish, but he was a hero in our household because of the way he knocked out the German, Max Schmeling, in one round in that great 1938 heavyweight championship fight in New York. I didn't see that one, but I listened on the radio. I still get chills thinking about it. My dad thought Louis was the greatest fighter who ever lived. I think that the thing about my life that would impress Dad the most was that I knew Joe.

Louis was a greeter at Caesars Palace when I knew him. He used to spend time at the Sahara Hotel health club, where I hung out. A nicer, kinder guy you'd never meet. He had a million friends around town, all of whom wanted to do things for him. I don't know how much money Caesars paid Joe, but he was so popular he could have lived well without a salary. Everybody wanted to cut him in on their action. He would have had a bundle if he'd been able to go to bed with money in his pocket, but he couldn't. What he didn't gamble away he gave to people with hard-luck stories.

Joe wasn't in the best of health in his later years. He suffered at least one serious stroke a year or so before he died, and it pretty much wiped him out. He also got kind of addicted to some of the medicines the doctors gave him to relieve his various ills.

Don't believe all that stuff you've heard about Joe being punchy before his health turned bad, though. He wasn't the world's smartest guy, but he'd been around and had a sly sense of humor. I remember that when Sonny Liston died in 1971, Joe and I were pallbearers at the funeral. We rode together in a limousine to the cemetery, and when the hearse passed through the gates, the policeman on duty saluted the procession. Joe looked at me, smiled, and said, "Sonny getting saluted by a cop! He would have gotten a kick out of that."

I knew Sonny Liston well; in fact, I was one of the few people he trusted. I guess that was because I was one of the few people who never wanted anything from him. Sonny was another fellow who was bum-rapped by just about everybody. To read the newspapers, you'd think he was some kind of a thug. He'd had a bad background, and he'd been in and out of trouble with the law all through his younger years. But after he became heavyweight champ he straightened himself out as best he could. It was just that his past never let go of him.

I first met Sonny in Las Vegas in 1962, after he'd kay-oed Floyd Patterson for the title. He lived in Denver then, but he trained some of the time in Las Vegas, and he later moved here. I'd see him around the hotels at first, and we'd talk boxing. Later, our wives got friendly and we'd all spend evenings together. Sonny was a guest in my home many times, and we'd visit him and his wife, Geraldine. I still have the medicine ball Sonny used when he trained.

Sonny was one of 24 brothers and sisters who grew up on a cotton farm outside of Little Rock, Arkansas. He was poor, and just about illiterate because he'd had very little schooling. He was a big, rough guy who made his money with what he had—his fists. He fought in the ring and out-side of it. He served a prison term for armed robbery, and he paid for that crime again and again because of the diffi-culties it caused him with the ring authorities. Several states, including New York, wouldn't license him to box because he'd done time, which I always thought was un-fair. Today, they even let guys with prison records play baseball!

Because Sonny was such a fearsome puncher, other fighters didn't want to meet him, so he had to take very bad money deals in order to get matches. Even when he was a contender, he'd have to fight for just 20 or 25 percent of a gate. I think that his difficulty in getting matches is what led him to hook up with some of the shady characters who used to manage him. They stole from him, too. He had very little to show for all the money he earned in the ring.

Sonny might never have had a chance to fight for the title if it hadn't been for President Kennedy. It seems that the president watched a boxing doubleheader on television in which Floyd Patterson, the champion, knocked out Tom McNeeley of Boston in one bout and Sonny knocked out Albert Westfall, a German, in the other. Kennedy later remarked to the press that the wrong two guys had fought that night. The remark got around and helped put the pressure on Patterson to give Sonny his shot. Sonny knocked out Patterson in the first round to win the title, and repeated the performance in the rematch.

I knew Sonny best after he'd lost his title to Muhammad Ali (he was called Cassius Clay then) in 1964 and moved to Las Vegas. He kept fighting after that, and I traveled with him to just about all of his later bouts. One trip we took that stands out in my mind—and says a lot about boxing, I think—was when Sonny fought Chuck Wepner in Jersey City, New Jersey, in 1967 or 1968.

The promoters of that fight were trying to build up Wepner for a bigger fight in New York, and did all they could to make sure he beat Sonny. They offered to set up training facilities for Sonny in New Jersey and then messed them up so that he couldn't train like he should. They put us up in a motel outside of Jersey City and told us we could eat there for free. After the first meal we looked for somewhere else to go; if the food wasn't poisoned, it sure was prepared by the world's worst cook! The night of the fight, one of the people who worked around the arena told us not to use the water bottle they'd give us for between rounds. We didn't know if the guy was on to anything, but we got our own water bottle just the same.

Wepner was a big white guy who'd had a good amateur record but was no great shakes as a pro. He was a bleeder to boot. Sonny knocked him around pretty good, and by the fourth or fifth round Wepner was all bloody. People were yelling to stop the fight. The doctor went into the ring to check the damage, and Wepner's handlers threw him out bodily. A round or two later even the referee couldn't help but notice the mess, and he finally stopped the fight. Later, one of the reporters asked Sonny if he thought Wepner was the bravest man he'd ever fought. "No, his manager was," Sonny replied. Who said that Sonny was dumb?

Not only was Sonny smarter than people gave him credit for, but his personal habits always were good as far as I knew. I never saw him drink liquor, and I'd swear in court that he wasn't a dope addict. When he was found dead in bed in his Las Vegas home in January of 1971, it was whispered that he had given himself an overdose of heroin, but I don't believe it. The story I heard was that he was after a couple of guys who had stiffed him in a business deal. They arranged somehow to get a meeting with him, and used it to slip him a mickey in a soft drink. When he was out they gave him the overdose. It was a sad end, but, I guess, it was inevitable for a man with Sonny's history.

As friendly as I was with Sonny, he never told me the true story of his one-round knockout by Ali in the famous rematch fight in Lewiston, Maine. Even when you're good friends with someone, you don't ask him about his women troubles or his downfall, and a downfall was what the second Ali fight was for Sonny. Amos "Big Train" Lincoln, Sonny's friend and sparring partner, told me after Sonny died that Sonny never was hurt by the punch that supposedly kayoed him. Lincoln said that Sonny was upset because he'd been hit with a federal income tax lien the day before the fight, and that threats had been made against his young stepdaughter, the daughter of his wife. Sonny just wanted to take the money and run, Lincoln said.

I don't know if Lincoln was right. When strangers asked Sonny what went wrong in Lewiston, he'd say, "Three things. Robert Goulet [the singer] forgot the words to the 'Star Spangled Banner.' Jersey Joe Walcott [the referee] missed the count [he must have counted to sixteen before he waved Sonny out]. And I never got up."

I always felt a bit bad about it, but there was something that I never told Sonny: that I made a nice score betting on the first Liston-Ali fight. I didn't actually bet against Sonny. I thought he'd win, just like everybody else did. In fact, Sonny was such a big favorite in that bout that it was hard to get down a straight win-or-lose bet. But I did bet that the fight would go four rounds, which it did (Sonny didn't come out for the seventh round).

Here's the story behind that. Sonny was training for the fight in Las Vegas and not working very hard. He had this kid with him named Sherman, who was a kind of mascot. Sherman would run with Sonny early in the morning on a Las Vegas golf course. I asked Sherman how many miles they'd been running. He said one or two. I knew that wasn't much for someone getting ready to fight a speedy guy like Ali.

I watched Sonny spar for that fight, and he took it pretty easy on his sparring partners. Most of them were friends of his, and he wasn't trying to hurt them. He took it easy in training generally for that fight. I guess he underestimated Ali. My reasoning in making my bet was that Ali was young and quick and probably could keep away from Sonny for four rounds. I never envisioned Sonny running out of gas and losing the way he did.

I won that bet, but I've lost some too. I've never kept sport-by-sport records, but I'm sure I'm not much better than even on boxing after a lifetime of betting on it. It's a tough sport to handicap even though its one-against-one nature makes it theoretically easier to figure than the team sports on which I do most of my wagering. You really never know how one man will do against another until he's done it.

They say that the fight game is more honest than it was in my days back in New York during the 1950s, when the gangsters just about ran it. I'm sure that it is, but that's not saying much. Team games are tough to fix because a player who's out there dumping is likely to get benched, but in boxing it's easy for a fighter to open himself to one good blow and take a convincing dive.

At the very least, you should make it your business to watch a fighter you want to bet on so you have some idea of his true ability. Taking a fighter because of a flashy record—especially a foreign fighter—is risky business.

There have been plenty of cases where guys with supposedly sterling won-lost marks in other countries were really busboys in local Mexican restaurants whose only serious bouts had been with the chefs.

You can't put a heck of a lot more trust in the ratings put out by the various organizations that oversee boxing—the World Boxing Association (WBA), World Boxing Council (WBC), and International Boxing Federation (IBF). Those outfits are political to the core, and they'll put a fighter in one of their divisional top tens if they think it'll help one of their allied promoters make a match.

I think that putting the government of boxing in the hands of those self-appointed groups is a crime. None of them has ever done a thing for the fighters. Boxing cries out for decent regulation, including making fighters prove their competence before they're allowed to enter the professional ring, verifying their records, making them take regular physical examinations, and putting aside a part of all gates for some kind of fighter pension plan. It's a mystery to me why the U.S. government hasn't led the way in this.

In boxing, your man not only has to win the fight for you to collect your bet, but he also may have to win the decision, which isn't always the same thing. I can't tell you how many bets I've lost on bum decisions. I'm especially susceptible to that because I usually bet on underdogs and in the vast majority of cases close decisions go to the favorite. The last time that happened to me was in the Larry Holmes–Carl "The Truth" Williams heavyweight title fight in the spring of 1985. I saw that fight on TV, and Williams, on whom I'd bet a small sum at 5 to 1 odds, had it won through 12 rounds. Holmes rallied to make it close, but I didn't think he caught the young challenger. Still, all three judges voted for the champ, and only one of them had the fight close. I wondered if they'd watched the same fight I did.

I've always thought that it would be good if the

round-by-round scores of the boxing judges were announced to the crowd—and the fighters—as a fight progressed. Boxing is one of the few sports where everyone is kept in the dark about who is winning until it's over. Announcing the scores after every round might subject officials to the kind of scrutiny they don't like, but that's a small price to pay for putting things out where everybody can see them. Judges couldn't go back and rejigger their cards to effect a certain outcome, and knowing he's behind or just slightly ahead might make a fighter stage a better bout in the late rounds. I think a lot of fighters come up short because they mistakenly think they are ahead in the late going, and coast.

Another thing that makes boxing a poor betting proposition is the way some of the Las Vegas books handle it. If a fight is rated even, you'll usually have to bet into odds of 11 to 10 *on either side.* The 11 to 10 odds make sense in football, where bettors divide their money among lots of games each weekend and it's tough for the house to balance its action. In a big fight (about the only kind that's posted for betting), there are just two alternatives, and balancing a book should be easier. A "nickel" line of $1.00 if you win, $1.05 if you lose, would be fairer. If you can believe it, some books may you lay 6 to 5 on either side in a pick 'em match. That's crazy for a bettor to take. There's always a lot of man-to-man action on the big fights, and my strong advice is that you find some if you can and avoid the vig.

Betting on boxing boils down to assessing the relative merits of two fighters, and I've never come across anyone who is better at it than Jimmy Grippo. He's got to be about 90 years old now, but he's still as sharp as they come. Jimmy lives in Las Vegas. He has been around boxing for most of his life and used to manage Melio Bettina, a light-heavyweight champion of the 1940s. Jimmy is a magician and hypnotist by trade. He performs in the side rooms at Caesars Palace Hotel. But he takes in every fight that comes to town and sometimes advises fighters' managers. He hypnotized Muhammad Ali before some of his fights, and he did the same for Jimmy Connors, the tennis player, when Connors had some big-money matches in town a few years ago. Grippo is a very respected guy.

Grippo has a great feel for boxing styles—which kinds of fighters can handle which other kinds. If I had followed his advice over the years, I'd have made a heckuva lot more money than I have. He picked out the Spinks brothers, Leon and Michael, as comers, and he was one of the few guys I knew who picked Ali over George Foreman in the famous rope-a-dope fight in Zaire. The huge Foreman took just two rounds each to kayo Joe Frazier and Ken Norton, both of whom had beaten Ali, and not many people (me included) thought that Ali could beat him. Jimmy pointed out that Frazier and Norton were straight-ahead fighters who walked right into Foreman's heavy punches, but that Ali was way too smart a fellow to do that. Boy, was he right!

Making money betting on boxing requires picking underdogs, and Jimmy has a good formula for identifying "live" ones. *He says that any fighter who is in good shape, can punch, and can take a punch can beat any other fighter.* That's about as simple as you can get. You might say that's not much to go on, and you'd be right. But in championship fights you're often talking about odds of 3, 4, or 5 to 1 against the challenger, and if you can hit on one of those every once in a while, you'll be golden.

One fight that Jimmy gave me was Leon Spinks over Ali in February of 1978. Leon had had only a half-dozen or so pro bouts going in, but Jimmy had him pegged that night, at least, as a rough customer who'd give 100 percent effort. At odds of 4 to 1, that was plenty good enough for me.

Jimmy also was instrumental in my betting on Marvin Hagler over Thomas Hearns in the big middleweight championship fight of 1985. Before the fight most of the press attention had been on the punching power of Hearns, who had knocked out almost all of his previous foes. But Jimmy pointed out that Hearns's kayo victims had been welterweights or junior middleweights, while Marvelous Marvin was a muscular, full-grown middleweight with a good knockout record of his own. In retrospect that sounds obvious, but it wasn't obvious to most of the people who bet on the fight and made Hearns the favorite up until the day of the bout.

My biggest boxing win I figured out myself, however. That was Larry Holmes over Ali in Las Vegas in 1980. I loved Holmes in that one from the day the fight was announced. Holmes came in at age 30 at the peak of his career. He was big, strong, and fast, and had a great jab. Ali was 38 years old and clearly past his prime. Like most fighters, he should have retired several years before he did, and now he's paying for it, poor guy.

Ali never worked too hard at training, but in getting ready for the Holmes fight he looked downright lethargic. He seemed to hesitate before hitting the heavy bag, and when he sparred he was just going through the motions, even though he made his typical jokes to conceal this. His weight was another thing against him. He had lost and gained a lot of pounds in the year or two before the bout, and while his weight was okay at fight time, all that reducing had to have taken its toll on him.

The only thing that bothered me about that fight was the rumor around town that things were fixed for Ali to win so that he and Holmes could have a rematch and another big payday. Yeah, they were fighting for the heavyweight championship of the world, and both fighters had never been anything but 100 percent honest as far as anyone knew. But this is boxing and you've got to pay attention to that sort of stuff.

My daughter had been doing some modeling at one of the dress salons in Caesars Palace, where Holmes and Ali were training, and she liked to spend her breaks watching them work out. She's a real boxing fan. One day she came home and told me about watching Holmes work. She said that right in the middle of things he grabbed a microphone and told the audience that he'd heard the rumors about the fix being in, and that they made him angry. Holmes reminded people that he was undefeated and had too much pride to go along with anything like that. He promised he would go all out to win.

That was all I needed to hear, and I turned my large bet into a very large one. Holmes had opened as an 8 to 5 favorite at most places around town, but as fight day approached more and more Ali money came in and the odds dropped to 6 to 5. I loved it. I remember the very last bet I made on Holmes. Gabe Kaplan, the comedian, was in line right behind me at the Caesars sports book. When he saw how much money I was betting his eyes bulged and he said, "Do you really like Holmes *that* much?" I told him it was the best investment I'd made in the last ten years. If you remember that fight, Holmes won every round before the referee stopped it in the eleventh.

The Holmes-Ali example brings up the subject of the rumors that surround every big fight. I try never to change my mind about a bet I plan to make because of the things I hear whispered. Most of them are nonsense that guys use to justify opinions that are really no more than stabs in the dark. I take notice, however, when all the rumors run in the same direction and when they come from reliable sources. In the Hagler-Hearns fight, for instance, I'd heard reports that Hearns had cut the inside of his mouth in training and that he'd been having trouble with muscle cramps in his legs. They met the above criteria, so I upped my bet on Hagler, whom I had liked all along. If I'd heard the same rumors about Hagler I'd still have bet him because I liked him on fundamentals, but I might have bet less than I did.

As I said before, I lose at least as many fight bets as I win, and it's a good thing that I don't depend on being right on boxing to make a living. I picked both of the Sugar Ray Leonard–Roberto Duran fights wrong and I lost a few bucks waiting for Holmes to fall to a younger man before Michael Spinks turned the trick in 1985. I'm glad to say that I had Spinks (at 5½ to 1!) in that one.

Meantime despite my setbacks, I'm always happy to read about a new big fight coming to town. There's nothing in sports like the atmosphere at one of those things. It's like a great big celebrity party where you see people you don't see very often. Everybody who's anybody shows up. I always feel like I'm lucky to be "invited."

7

MONEY
MANAGEMENT

You might find this hard to believe, but it's easier to pick winners in sports than it is to come out ahead financially. If I had a dollar for every smart guy who came to Las Vegas looking to score, and left broke because he didn't know how to manage his money, I'd be eating caviar for breakfast every morning. The vigorish may be the bookmaker's best friend, but bettor weakness, greed, and fear are right up there as close friends.

A classic Las Vegas joke makes the point. It's about a gambler who's on his last legs moneywise. He goes to see his friend the betting maven and practically gets on his knees asking the guy to give him a winner.

"Okay," says the maven. "I've got a basketball game for you. Three of one of the team's starters are hurt and nobody knows about it but me. The coach is my nephew and he says there's no way his team can win. If that's not enough, the referee is my brother-in-law, and he's in my pocket. As much as you want to win, that's how much you can bet against this team."

"Great," says the down-and-outer. "Now give me another team so I can make a parley."

There's more truth than humor in that story, and I'm talking about professionals, too, not just amateurs. Nobody who hasn't had some initial success in gambling tries to make a living at it; in other words, all pros start out as winners. That all but a small handful of them wind up broke is testimony to their inability to control their egos and emotions when it comes to handling their bankrolls. Women, booze, and late hours knock off a lot of gamblers, but bad money management remains number one on the hit parade.

The biggest mistake a gambler can make is to try to play catch-up by increasing his bets when he falls behind. Everybody—and that includes me—has bad streaks. If you up your bets in an attempt to get even fast, it'll be like you're in quicksand: the more you struggle, the deeper in you'll get. Nearly as bad is the inability to take advantage of winning streaks to earn the kind of money that makes gambling really worthwhile financially.

You should understand that when I talk about winning and losing streaks, *I'm not talking strictly about luck.* A winning bettor is a confident bettor. He makes his selections fully expecting to win. He isn't plagued by the doubts and second thoughts that afflict people having so-so success. I believe he has the powerful, positive frame of mind that allows him to pick winners almost by accident. When you're in that groove, you should be smart and brave enough to capitalize on it.

Losing, of course, has exactly the opposite effect. A losing streak can make someone back away from good choices because of uncertainty. The loser watches games waiting for disaster to strike, and, somehow, it usually does. That's all the more reason to cut back on your bets when you're behind. Gamblers should understand the psychology of both winning and losing so that they can deal with the swings of fortune that they'll surely experience.

I think it's important to look at the financial side of sports betting with *realistic expectations*. You should realize that gambling isn't the easiest way in the world to make a buck; if it were, everybody would be rich. Nobody wins all of the time, or even nearly all of the time. Nobody breaks the bank at Monte Carlo. I'd estimate that my lifetime winning percentage is around 60 percent. I put in 70 hours a week on my bets. Don't you expect to do better gambling on sports as a hobby.

Betting into the 11 to 10 bookmaker's vig on football and basketball makes coming out ahead in the long run a tough, tough proposition. Say that you made 100 bets of $100 each on professional football over the course of a season, and that you won on 58 of them—a very nice winning percentage. You'd collect $5,800 (58 × $100) on your victories, and lose $4,620 (42 × $110) on the games you dropped. That would be a profit of $1,180.

Now let's say that you won 42 bets and lost 58, which is every bit as likely statistically as a 58–42 mark. Your 42 wins would net you $4,200 (42 × $100) and your 58 losses would cost you $6,380 (58 × $110). That's a net loss of $2,180. Quite a difference, huh? That's what they mean when they say that the odds are against you.

Don't get grandiose. Try to gauge your wagers so that if you win over a season you'll make enough money to buy yourself a new set of golf clubs or take your wife on a weekend vacation somewhere. If you lose, keep your losses to where you can shrug them off. Look at sports betting the way you would a country-club membership. If you enjoy the games and the action, a little cost shouldn't bother you. If you win, think of it as a bonus.

It's also important that you understand the range of

bets that a gambler can make on sports. They aren't all equally attractive. As far as I'm concerned, the most sensible bet is the straight, one-game wager into the 11 to 10 odds with the points on football or basketball, or into the baseball "dime" line. It's difficult to pick a winner, and when I do I want to see the cash in my pocket. The bookmakers offer a number of other betting propositions, though, and you should know their pros and cons.

PARLAY CARDS

These make you pick three or more consecutive winners to collect, and for my money (which the card boys don't get), they are all "con." The simple reason is that their payoffs don't nearly justify the risk.

The typical parlay card pays $6 for $1 on three winners in as many picks, $11 for $1 for four, $20 for $1 for five, $40 for $1 for six, $80 for $1 for seven, $150 for $1 for eight, $300 for $1 for nine, and $500 for $1 for ten. Some also pay $25 for $1 if you can pick nine winners in ten choices.

You probably noticed right away that these odds are stated in terms of 6 *for* 1, etc. In normal betting, if you win at odds of 6 to 1 you get your dollar back plus $6.00, or a total of $7.00. Six *for* one means that you just get back $6.00, which is really 5 to 1. That's no bargain.

Ties lose—another atrocity against the bettor—and the true odds against being perfect on between 3 and 10 picks are much greater than the parlay-card payoffs. To find the true odds, you have to multiply .5, or ½, by how many games you are choosing. The odds of picking three winners in three tries are $\frac{1}{2} \times \frac{1}{2} \times \frac{1}{2}$, or $\frac{1}{8}$. That works out to 8 to 1. The true odds on picking six straight winners are 64 to 1, while the cards only pay off at 35 for 1. The deal gets worse as you go up the ladder.

The books love the cards because the profits on them are huge. The runners—the guys who hustle them on the streets—get a 50 percent commission on everything they sell. With commissions like that, you can imagine your chances of winning.

TEASERS

Teaser bets are the books' way to get you to make serious win-parlay bets on two or more teams. The enticement, or "teaser," is that they give you 6, 6½, or 7 points to use any way you want on the teams you pick in football, or 4½ points in basketball.

If you take two teams with the 6-point teaser in football, you get an even-money bet instead of the 11 to 10 you have to lay on single game wagers. With 6½ points, you lay the usual 11 to 10 odds. With 7 points, you have to lay 6 to 5.

Here's an example of how a football teaser works. Say that the Rams are 9-point favorites over the Giants and the Chargers are 7-points over the Patriots. If you take the 6-point teaser, you can take the Rams minus-3 or the Giants plus-15, and the Chargers minus-1 or the Pats plus-13. You do the same plus-minus arithmetic with the 6½ or 7 points, only the odds are different. Basketball works the same, except that most books only allow the 4½ (or, sometimes, 4) points on two teams, with the bettor laying 11 to 10. A tie on any side of a teaser scratches the entire bet in both football and basketball.

I don't like teaser wagering. In the first place, teasers have become a worse proposition for the bettor than they used to be. In basketball, the books used to give you 6 points to play with, but they whittled that down. In college football, they stuck with the 6-, 6½-, and 7-point line even after the 2-point conversion came along and made those numbers meaningless as "keys." If they wanted to be fair, the books would offer 7-, 7½-, and 8-point teasers on college football. But, of course, they're in business to make money, not to be fair, and most of them do it very well. My second objection is that, no matter how you fiddle with the points, with a teaser bet you've got to win two games to be paid off like you would for one winner in normal betting. That's not a good proposition by me.

I do, however, make occasional teaser wagers. I play them mostly during the NFL playoffs, which are must-win games where ties aren't allowed. I'll usually take teams that I consider to be strong favorites and reduce the points on them *if I can get their numbers below one of my keys.*

Say that the Miami Dolphins are a 7½-point favorite in a playoff game. I might take it in a two-team, 7-point teaser and knock its spread down to a half-point. There's no such thing as a half-point game, so all I'd really be betting on in that half of the bet is that Miami wins the game.

Or say that I like Pittsburgh and it's a 9-point pick. I might use it in a 6½-point teaser, knocking its number down to 2½. That would give me a half-win if the Steelers won by a field goal, or 3 points. That's a key number because it's a common margin of victory in the pros.

Like I said, I usually refuse to be teased—at least, not by the bookies.

OVER-AND-UNDER

In over-and-under wagering, you bet on whether the *total number of points scored* in a game will be above or below the number posted by the books. They usually get their number by taking the average number of points scored in the previous games involving each team, adding them together, and dividing by 2.

Say that the Chiefs are playing Tampa Bay. The Chiefs have scored 18 points a game and allowed 24 for a total of 42. The Buccaneers have scored 21 a game and allowed 30 for a total of 51. So, 42 plus 51 equals 93, divided by 2 is 46½. That'd probably be the number. If you bet the "under," you'd win if the total score was 46 points or less. You'd win the "over" if the total score topped 47 points. It works the same way in basketball.

Over-and-under is getting to be a popular form of wagering, especially on the Monday night pro games, when the books have only one other item to sell. I really can't explain its popularity. As far as I'm concerned, it's a pure guess, and you're giving the usual 11 to 10.

I suppose that a couple of things *could* give a bettor an edge on the over-and-under. One would be the weather: if it's bad, scoring usually is lower than normal. The trouble is, bookies can call the weather bureau just like bettors can, and they'll usually drop their number if snow or heavy rain is forecast. The same goes for injuries to key players. My advice: don't get involved with this bet unless you're willing to do your homework.

MIDDLES

A "middle" occurs when a bettor takes advantage of changes in a point spread—or differences in the spreads of two bookmaking establishments—to win *both sides* of a wager. Catching a middle has been compared to filling an inside straight in poker or having a multiple orgasm. In other words, it's wonderful.

The most famous middle in recent football history came in the 1979 Super Bowl game between the Pittsburgh Steelers and Dallas Cowboys. The Steelers opened as a 3½-point favorite, and then went to 4 points and 4½ points. It closed right on the number 4, which is what Pittsburgh won by, 35–31.

Just about everybody who bet on the game either won or tied, and people who gave the 3½ points on the Steelers and took the 4½ (there weren't as many as claimed to have done it, but more than a few) hit a middle. You could have heard the Las Vegas bookies howl as far away as Los Angeles if your window had been open! They compared that day to Pearl Harbor, the sinking of the *Maine,* and the crash of 1929 all rolled into one. One bookie's natural-blond girlfriend disguised herself by dyeing her roots black and ran away with a winning bettor. As far as I was concerned, it couldn't have happened to a nicer bunch of guys.

A more typical example of a middle involves a 2-point gap in the spread. A team might be favored by 7 points at one book and 5 at another. You'd lay the 5 and take the 7. If your team wins by 6 points, you'd collect on both bets. If it wins by 5, that's not bad, either, because you'd tie that one and collect on the 7. If it wins by 7, you'd tie the 7-pointer and win the 5. So, really, you have 3 points working for you—the 5, 6, and 7.

The trouble is (and in gambling there's *always* a catch when a proposition looks too good) you don't find as many opportunities for middles as you used to. Just about all the books have access to the same information now, and their football and basketball lines rarely vary by more than a point.

Moreover, if you try to catch a middle and fail, you'll be a net loser because of the vig if you bet equal amounts of money on both sides. I figure that the odds against catching a true middle with a 3-point difference—the smallest gap worth making a shot worthwhile—are 20 to 1. You can go a long time without hitting on one of those. That's mainly why I long ago stopped chasing middles. And on the infrequent occasions when I do take both sides of a bet, I'll always wager heaviest on the side of my own numbers so I'll be rewarded if my basic judgment is correct. That way, if I do get the middle, it's gravy.

HOW TO BET

Now let's get down to the basics: how to handle your bankroll. I can't give you any set dollar amounts because everyone's circumstances are different. I'm in gambling to make a living, so I have to bet heavily. I'll rarely make a wager of less than $1,000, and I've been known to put more than $50,000 on a game or fight. But don't be too impressed by those figures. It's not what you wager that counts, but the amount that sticks on one side or the other. Over the course of a year, you'll probably win or lose less than 10 percent of the money that goes back and forth across the windows.

Before you begin a sports-gambling season, you should put aside a sum of money that you can afford to lose comfortably. Everybody's comfort level is different, so you should look at it this way: *you know you've bet too much when you're not happy that you've won, just relieved that you didn't lose.* Whatever you do, don't bet the rent money. It's hard to come out ahead financially in gambling under any circumstances; no one needs the extra pressure that comes with betting what gamblers call "tough money." I think that one reformed pro I know, who now bets only for fun, put it best when he told me, "I'm doing a lot better now that I don't *have* to win."

Once you've set aside your roll, resolve not to risk more than 5 percent of it on any single game, or more than 25 percent in any day. If you stick to that rule, your bets will rise and fall with your fortunes. That's the only proper way to go about things.

Say, for instance, that you want to bet on professional football, and that you decide you can afford to lose $2,000 over the season without flinching. That would mean that—to start—you would bet no more than $100 a game (of course, you could bet less) or $500 on any Sunday. Now say that you win seven bets and lose three in the first two weeks of the season. That would give you a net gain of $370 and bring your bankroll to $2,370. You could raise your maximum single-game bet to $120, and your Sunday limit to $600.

If your luck holds as the season wears on, you'll be able to finish with a flourish. Say that you're $1,000 to $1,500 ahead when the playoffs begin. You'd be able to bet $300 to $500 a game in the last few weeks *while still preserving your original capital.* That's what I mean by taking advantage of your success.

If, on the other hand, you are not so lucky, reducing your bets in line with my 5 percent and 25 percent rules at least will keep you in the game until the end. You never can tell when your luck might change, and if you're tapped out, you won't be able to salvage anything when it does. Do like a smart baseball player in a hitting slump does: choke up on your bat (bankroll) and try just to make contact. The hits will start to come.

Remember, they play the "Star Spangled Banner" every day, and you'll want to be ready for action when they do. Survival is the name of the game. The poet Oliver Goldsmith must have been a gambler. In 1761 he wrote:

> *For he who fights and runs away*
> *May live to fight another day;*
> *But he who is in battle slain*
> *Can never rise to fight again.*

I couldn't put it better myself.

(My football bankroll example doesn't hold for betting on basketball and baseball. If you want to tackle these sports seriously, I'd suggest an initial stake about four times what you'd set aside for football, and a 2 percent per game betting limit. Basketball and baseball come at you every day, and you have to be faster on your feet than you are for the weekends-only game of football. You'll have less time to ponder your losses and, more important, let your ego heal between rounds. Betting on basketball and baseball is like psychoanalysis. It's for the healthy and wealthy.)

GETTING VALUE

How much you should bet on any particular game is a question of value. The more you like a game, the more you should want to risk on it. Don't leave this decision to impulse or emotion. Let the numbers—yours and the bookmakers'—determine the size of your wagers.

You can get value in two ways: by shopping the odds, and by understanding the "key number" theory I've referred to several times earlier. I can't overemphasize the importance of either.

I put in 70 hours a week on my bets, and more than half that time goes into canvassing the local bookmakers' spreads. I have a team of guys on the Strip who stick their noses into every betting establishment several times a day and phone me when lines change. I'm like a housewife who knows the price of coffee in every supermarket in town. And when I see a bargain, I pounce!

My motto on value is this: *what you save is what you earn.* I honestly believe that, for a guy who bets as much as I do, the point I pick up here and the half-point there can make the difference between winning and losing over the course of a year. It sometimes takes patience to wait until the line gets to where I want it before I bet, and many's the time I have passed on a bet that my heart wanted to make because I couldn't get the right number. But I wouldn't be here to write this book if I didn't have the discipline it takes to restrain myself.

You'll say, sure, Banker can talk about shopping because he's in Las Vegas where there are a hundred places to bet. You've probably got only two or three outlets, or maybe just one. Still, you can shop the outlets you have, and you shouldn't be shy about asking your bookie to give you a half-point once in a while. If you're a good customer, and you don't owe him anything, he may surprise you by saying yes. The worst that can happen is that he'll say no.

You also can look for guys to make man-to-man bets with—that way you can avoid the vigorish altogether. I do that quite a bit. Just make sure that the fellow you bet with has a good reputation for paying when he loses. That,

I'm sorry to say, is a subject I could write another whole book on.

The amount of money I'll bet on a game depends on the difference between my number and the bookmakers' line. Obviously, the wider the gap, the more I'll wager. In professional football, my "key number" theory is very much a part of my betting system. To repeat, the usual key numbers in the pros are 3, 4, 6, 7, 10, 14, and 17 points. Those are the margins by which many games are decided.

Say that I make the Raiders a 6-point choice over the Rams. If the line is the Raiders minus-5, I'd definitely pass because 5 is a "dead" number—one by which few games are decided. If it's Raiders minus-4, I'd make a routine bet on the Raiders. If it's Raiders minus-3, I'd bet more substantially. If it's Raiders minus-2½, the Raiders probably would be one of my strongest bets of the day.

Now let's go the other way. If the line is Raiders plus-7, I might make a small bet on the Rams. Plus-7½ definitely would warrant a wager. An 8-point spread wouldn't entice me to bet further because 8, like 5, is a dead number. I might up my bet on the Rams a bit at 9, because, while it's not a "key," a 9-point margin occurs sometimes. At Raiders plus-10, I'd *love* the Rams.

In college football, I look for a wider difference—3½ points—before I bet initially. The pros' key numbers don't hold in the colleges because of the 2-point conversion and easier field goals due to the wider goal posts (they're 23 feet 4 inches wide in the colleges and 18 feet 6 inches wide in the pros). I usually look for further jumps of 2½ points or more before I'll risk more than a routine wager on a college team. Still, with 50 or so major-college games to choose from every week, I usually find plenty of opportunities to keep my money busy on autumn Saturdays.

One last note: it's a good idea to keep records of your bets. You'll need them in case you have an argument with the fellows you bet with, and it's good to be able to go back and check your picks during a season so you can see where you went right, or wrong. If you're a pro, of course, you'll need records for the tax man.

One more last note: don't be afraid to pass a game. In fact, don't be afraid to pass lots of games. Just because you plan to watch a game on television doesn't mean you have to bet. Save your hard-earned bucks for the games your numbers tell you to play.

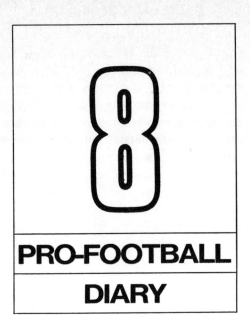

PRO-FOOTBALL
DIARY

It's Monday, September 2, 1985—Labor Day. I'm sitting by my pool in my bathing suit, enjoying the sun. I just had a swim and I feel great. The National Football League season starts this Sunday, September 8, and I'm up for it.

I remember 1957—my first year in Las Vegas. I couldn't get over the fact that the temperature was in the seventies and eighties all through October and November, when the football season was in full swing. Football just didn't seem right without leaves on the ground and a chill in the air. I've gotten used to it since, though. Who says you can't be happy in a place where the weather is nice?

Another reason I'm happy is that I wiped out the bookmakers (well, almost) by going 14–5, or 74 percent winners, in the NFL preseason. As I explained in chapter 3, my key was a 4–0 record on the Chicago Bears. The Bears' coach, Mike Ditka, told the newspapers what he would do before every game, and then he went and did it. That's my kind of coach. Winning in the preseason, of course, means that I start the regular campaign with the bookies' money in my pocket, which means that I can bet heavier than I might otherwise in the first few weeks.

This is the first entry in a diary of the 1985 NFL season that I will keep for this book. I'll record all the bets I make, my reasons for making them, and their outcomes. My purpose is to show how I apply the football-betting guidelines I laid down in chapter 3. I'll also make some points about money management that will be applicable to betting on all sports.

Now, I know what you are thinking. "What's to keep Banker from changing history if he has to in order to make himself look good?" It's a question you should ask. The first part of the answer is that I'm an honest guy. To make it as a gambler, you have to be honest with yourself and the people you bet with. Also, my livelihood depends on my winning, and the local department stores would know pretty quick if I hit a bad streak because they wouldn't be seeing my wife so often. As it is, she supports them.

The second part of my answer is that there are plenty of people around Las Vegas who know how I bet. They are the people who own and work in the sports books, and the 50 or so friends who call me every week to get my picks so they can follow them. I never hesitate to tell my friends how I have bet once I get my money down and the line changes can't hurt me. These people, in turn, tell others. It's not uncommon for me to be walking along the Strip and have a perfect stranger come up and congratulate me on a win or kid me about a loss the weekend before.

In addition, I appear several times a year on a Saturday-night radio show that my friend, Lee Pete, runs from the Stardust Hotel. He gets a bunch of handicappers together, and we go over our NFL picks for the next day. The program is heard all over Southern California as well as in Nevada. That means a couple hundred thousand people know who I like some weeks.

The only caution I think I have to add concerns the point spreads I bet into. As I have said in previous chapters, one of the big reasons I do well is my willingness to shop the lines and wait until I get my number before putting down my money. I have a team of fellows who are on the Strip all day scouting lines for me. I may say that I took the Packers with 4 points in a certain game, for example, when all you might have been able to get were 3 or 3½ points. That would be a case where my shopping paid off. I keep betting receipts for the tax boys to check (which they do), so I stand ready to document every bet I describe.

The 1985 NFL season starts with four new coaches on board: Rod Dowhower of the Indianapolis Colts, Darryl Rogers of the Detroit Lions, Leeman Bennett of the Tampa Bay Buccaneers, and Bud Grant of the Minnesota Vikings. Marty Schottenheimer of the Cleveland Browns and Raymond Berry of the New England Patriots begin their first full seasons, each having coached their teams for the last eight games of 1984.

Of all the new coaches, the only one I will alter my power rating for is Grant of the Vikings. He coached that club with generally excellent results for 17 seasons before stepping down for a year while Les Steckel took charge. Grant is an easygoing type; Steckel tried to run the team along military lines. The result of Grant's leaving was pure disaster. I'll take 2 points off my Vike's rating in Grant's honor. I'm from Missouri on the rest.

Here's my general rundown on all 28 NFL teams as the new season opens. In parentheses after each team's name is its 1984 won-lost record for all games, including playoffs, and its record against the point spread.

Atlanta Falcons (4-12, 4-12 versus spread) I
think the Falcons helped themselves in the off-season by
drafting huge offensive tackle Bill Fralic out of Pitt and
getting wide receiver Charley Brown in trade from Washington. This team still is shaky, though, and I don't look for
any major improvement.

Buffalo Bills (2-14, 5-10) The Bills' offense seems
a bit improved with Vince Ferragamo at quarterback and
Greg Bell, who had a good rookie season last year, at running back. The defense remains just fair and I don't think
they'll improve much from their worst in the league mark
of last year.

Chicago Bears (11-7, 10-8) This is a team that
stacks up best where I think it counts most: on the ground.
It has the league's best running attack and the best defense
against the run. The Bears certainly figure to make the
playoffs. How they do once they get there will depend on
whether quarterback Jim McMahon stays healthy and
coach Ditka can handle the team under pressure.

Cincinnati Bengals (8-8, 9-6) I think Kenny Anderson has had it at quarterback. Coach Sam Wyche
should bench him for veteran backup Turk Schonert or
second-year-man Boomer Esiason. The defensive backfield
is weak, but their talent otherwise is pretty good. This
ought to be a competitive team but not a top one.

Cleveland Browns (5-11, 9-6) This team had a
good defense but not much offense last season. With two
new quarterbacks (vet Gary Danielson from Detroit and
rookie Bernie Kosar) and a lack of good wide receivers, I
don't expect its personality to change. The Browns' won-
lost record should be close to .500, but they'll be a decent
underdog pick because they'll play a lot of close games.

Dallas Cowboys (9-7, 7-8) The Cowboys had a rare off-year in 1984, but I don't expect them to have another this time. Coach Landry says he'll go with Danny White at quarterback from the start, and stability at QB should help. The offensive line isn't the power it used to be, but the defense still looks strong. I think they'll be a playoff team again.

Denver Broncos (13-4, 11-6) The Broncos did it with mirrors and opponents' turnovers last year. They won 10 more games than they lost in the regular season while being outgained by their opponents overall! Quarterback John Elway should be improved in his third season. The defense is good, and, as always, the Broncos should be tough at home in Mile High Stadium. They have no real running game, though, and I don't look for them to match their 1984 mark.

Detroit Lions (4-11-1, 6-10) New coach Rogers was no great success at Arizona State, his last job, and I think that Joe Ferguson, the veteran quarterback the Lions got in trade from Buffalo, is worse than Danielson, the quarterback they traded to Cleveland. The Lions didn't look good in the preseason. At best, they figure to win a game or two more than last year.

Green Bay Packers (8-8, 8-7) The Packers came on strong at the end of 1984, winning seven of their last eight games, mostly because of an improved defense. Quarterback Lynn Dickey isn't getting any better or younger at age 36, though, and I can't see them as a contender this season.

Houston Oilers (3-13, 4-11) This is a young team that figures to improve. The offense should get better as a young line matures and quarterback Warren Moon, out of the Canadian league, gets used to the NFL. I think they'll win a few more games than last year, and cover a few more times.

Indianapolis Colts (4-12, 7-9)   I don't look for any quick improvement from the Colts under new coach Dowhower, but he ought to have better rapport with his players than tough-guy Frank Kush did. This team has an okay running game, but no passing to speak of and a poor defense. Still a bad team.

Kansas City Chiefs (8-8, 8-8)   The Chiefs showed signs of breaking out of mediocrity in the last three games of 1984 when they beat Denver, Seattle, and San Diego. Maybe they're ready to contend. Pluses include their passing game, pass rush, and kicking. More progress depends on an improved running attack.

Los Angeles Raiders (11-5, 7-9)   The Raiders are a great organization that always finds a way to win, even though they weren't a great bet in 1984. They're solid in both rushing offense and defense. They're getting old in spots, and quarterbacks Jim Plunkett and Marc Wilson lack mobility. Even so, they'll still be playing in January.

Los Angeles Rams (10-7, 8-9)   The Rams are like the Bears in that they're tough on both sides of the running game, which makes them a sure plus-.500 team in my book. Negatives include front-office problems and a 34-year-old "rookie" quarterback in Dieter Brock from the Canadian league. If they make the playoffs, they don't figure to get far.

Miami Dolphins (16-3, 12-6)   The Dolphins were clearly the second-best team in the NFL last year. Their passing game, with Dan Marino at quarterback, was one of the best in league history and was good enough to make up for a so-so running attack and an only slightly better than average defense. I look for running-game improvement this season when rookie running backs Lorenzo Hampton from Florida and Ron Davenport from Louisville work themselves into the lineup. The Dolphins had preseason contract problems with Marino and some key defensive players. If those get settled, as they should, I see nothing to keep them from contending strongly again.

Minnesota Vikings (3-13, 5-11) This will be a happier team with coach Grant back, and a better one as a result of the acquisition of wide receiver Anthony Carter, formerly of the U.S. Football League. The Vikings aren't what they used to be, but they should add a few wins.

New England Patriots (9-7, 6-10) There has been something lacking in this team for the last several years, and I admit that I don't know what it is. The Patriots can beat the best teams and lose to the worst ones. Despite their good offensive line, and a good, young passer in quarterback Tony Eason, I'm always nervous about playing them.

New Orleans Saints (7-9, 7-9) The Saints are no great team to start with, and they've got more problems with preseason injuries to a couple of starting offensive linemen. I think that their number one quarterback, Richard Todd, is a stiff, and his backups, Dave Wilson and Bobby Herbert, are unproven. They'll be a long-spread underdog all season.

New York Giants (10-8, 8-10) They made the playoffs last year, and I think they will again this time. They have the best group of linebackers in the league, and solid runners in little Joe Morris and big Rob Carpenter. Phil Simms is a better than average quarterback, but his receivers aren't as good as he is. I see this team playing and winning a lot of close games. I won't give big points on them.

New York Jets (7-9, 6-9) I look for improvement here with Ken O'Brien installed as a regular quarterback and Freeman O'Neill healthy again at running back. Defense looks good. Question marks are a couple of contract holdouts in the offensive line and Joe Walton's coaching ability. If Walton doesn't win, he's through—maybe before the season is out.

Philadelphia Eagles (6-9-1, 10-6) A lot of problems here. The new owner, Norman Braman, wants to reduce his payroll, and I'm sure he's got a fishy eye on his holdover coach, Marion Campbell. Defense looks okay, but the offense lacks punch. I see no great won-lost improvement, but nine of the Eagles' 10 point-spread wins last year came as underdogs, so I have to respect them with the points.

Pittsburgh Steelers (10-8, 9-9) The Steelers don't look terrific on paper, but they didn't last year, either, and they made it to the AFC championship game. Also, they were the only team to beat San Francisco. Only slightly better than average in all departments, but Chuck Noll is a great coach.

St. Louis Cardinals (9-7, 9-7) Potentially, the Cardinals have the best all-around offense in football with quarterback Neil Lomax, speedy receiver Roy Green, and running back Otis Anderson. They'll be Super Bowl prospects if their defense improves just a notch. As a betting proposition, they may be overpriced early in the season because of all the news-media attention they've been getting.

San Diego Chargers (7-9, 8-8) As usual, the Chargers should score a lot of points, and so should their opponents. Quarterback Dan Fouts has about the quickest passing release in the game. That's fortunate, because with his team's aging offensive line, he'd get killed otherwise. This is a tough team to bet on, or against. The Chargers are a gamble every week.

San Francisco 49ers (18-1, 14-5) Defending Super Bowl champ; great team; no obvious weaknesses. The only minus apparent now is the historical one that it's tough to repeat as champ in any professional sport these days. Also, the 49ers have become a "public" team like the Cowboys and Raiders, so bettors will have to give up big points to get them.

Seattle Seahawks (13-5, 11-6) The Seahawks are the St. Louis Cardinals of the AFC: they're the darlings of the press in the preseason. I'm not so sure they're Super Bowl material. They are sound on both offense and defense, and their offense could be very good if running back Curt Warner is recovered from his knee surgery. But the key to their good showing last year was their defense's ability to get turnovers, and I don't think they can count on that again. Their coach, Chuck Knox, has shown he can take teams to the playoffs, but he has yet to make a Super Bowl appearance. He's too conservative for my taste, and I don't think he'll make it this year.

Tampa Bay Buccaneers (6-10, 10-5) This was another screwy team in 1984—a loser on the field, and a winner at the windows. Seven of the Bucs' 10 point-spread victories were as underdogs. They're a question mark this year. Their offense looks good with Steve DeBerg at quarterback and James Wilder running and catching passes. Their defense is suspect. I think a lot will depend on what kind of start they get.

Washington Redskins (11-6, 9-7) This is *my* choice to go all the way. Joe Theismann is a great quarterback operating behind a great offensive line. Riggins should have one more good year in him, and the acquisition of George Rogers from New Orleans gives them a great running back in reserve if Riggins can't do it. The Redskins have no stars on defense, but a lot of good players who get the job done. With all their veterans, this may be their last year on top. But I think they'll make the best of it.

REGULAR SEASON

WEEK 1

I did my homework as usual, and on Saturday night, September 7, I was on the Lee Pete radio show, ready with my picks. The sports book at the Stardust Hotel was packed with my friends and enemies, and they all had their pencils ready. I'd come off a great preseason, and they couldn't wait to follow me to the bank.

The same went for the other professionals on the panel. When I disagreed with one of their selections, they'd back off and switch to my side. I tell you, it was a real ego trip.

I came down with a crash the next day. I was 0 for 6! It was my worst week since I went 0 for 9 one week during the 1981 season. My wife wouldn't talk to me on Monday, and there was a movement on the Strip to hang me in effigy, or in person if that could be arranged. The only ones who still liked me were my cats and dog, and then only at feeding time. Here's a chronicle of the disaster.

THE LOSSES:

Miami minus-7 at Houston I thought the price was right even though Miami quarterback Marino had signed a new contract and started practicing only the week before. If he couldn't play, I figured the powerful Dolphins would win with backup QB Don Strock. Houston won straight up, 26–23.

Atlanta minus-2½ at home versus Detroit   I had the Falcons minus-2, but I became opinionated and took them at 2½. Detroit played some awful games in the pre-season, and I figured the Falcons would have enough muscle to win at home. Atlanta led by 14 at one point, but lost, 28–27.

Cincinnati plus-3 at home versus Seattle   This was the first test of my Seattle-is-overrated theory, and it cost me. The Bengals fell 4 points behind early, and couldn't make it up. They had a couple of opportunities to get within 1 point with field goals in the fourth quarter, but went for touchdowns instead and failed both times. Seattle won, 28–24.

Green Bay plus-5 at New England   My figures had this game a toss-up. I figured the Packers had enough offense and defense to stay close to the Patriots, if not win. Green Bay fell behind early and couldn't catch up. A Pats' safety in the second half doomed me to still another 1-point loss, 26–20.

New York Jets plus-10 at Los Angeles Raiders   I knew the Jets were hurting in their offensive line, where two regulars hadn't signed new contracts. That's something that usually turns me off of a team. I guess I'm a sucker for a pair of pretty legs and 10-point underdogs. The Raiders dominated in the trenches and blew out the Jets, 31–0.

Washington plus-1 at Dallas   I loved this Monday night game selection. The Redskins were my pick to win the Super Bowl, and I thought that their huge offensive line would dominate. Wouldn't you know it, they fell behind early, and the Cowboys' defense never let them get back in the game. The Cowboys romped, 44–14.

RECORD TO DATE: 0 WINS, 6 LOSSES

WEEK 2

I went into this week with the dubious consolation of knowing I couldn't do much worse than last week. My friends and followers were counting on me for a bailout. I did my darnedest, but came out 3–3. I still felt like an outcast and second-class citizen.

THE WINS:

Detroit (1-0) plus-5 at home against Dallas (1-0)   I finally won a game. This selection was the direct result of Dallas being overpriced as a result of their big win over traditional rival Washington the Monday night before. The game also illustrated my point about the importance of emotion in the professional game: the Cowboys were due for a letdown after their big Washington effort. The Lions did everything right for more than a half, taking a 26–0 lead. They held on to win, 26–21, even though the Cowboys would be the superior team in three games out of four between them.

New York Jets (0-1) minus-3½ at home against Buffalo (0-1)   I made this game Jets minus-6½. That's a big gap with the spread in the pros, so I bet heavily. I knew that the Bills were weak and that the Jets, with their offensive-line holdouts back, were better than their horrible opening-game loss. The Jets won, 42–3.

Green Bay (0–1) plus-1 at home versus the New York Giants (1–0)   This was another emotional-factors pick. The Packers were going to honor their heroes of the Vince Lombardi era at the game, and I thought that the team and the crowd would get properly worked up. The Packers won, 23–20, even though the Giants looked like the better team.

THE LOSSES:

Tampa Bay (0–1) minus-3 at home against Minnesota (1–0)   I liked the Bucs here even though the Vikings had upset the 49ers by a point the week before, while the Bucs were losing to the Bears, 38–28. I thought their offense was stronger than the Vikings'. I watched the game on TV, and Tampa Bay could have opened a bakery with all its turnovers. The Vikes won, 31–16.

Philadelphia (0–1) plus-5 at home against the Los Angeles Rams (1–0)   The Eagles went with rookie quarterback Randall Cunningham, but I thought their defense would keep them close. One bad call by an official turned the game around. Cunningham was stripped of the ball inside his own 10-yard line, and the Rams recovered and scored. The TV replays showed that it was an incomplete pass. The Rams won, 17–6.

New Orleans (0–1) plus-10 at Denver (0–1)   This was a frustrating one to lose. I watched the Saints fall behind and make a determined comeback. They got to 34–23 with more than 8 minutes left and had several opportunities to kick a field goal and cut the margin to 8. They went for touchdowns each time and came up empty. Final score, 34–23. It was my third 1-point loss in two weeks. Ugh!

RECORD TO DATE: 3 WINS, 9 LOSSES

WEEK 3

This was the kind of week handicappers dream about. I went 8 and 1, and the only game I lost I should have won. My two biggest bets—on Miami and Pittsburgh—both prevailed. I'm now in the black for the regular season at the won-lost column and, more important, at the cash window.

THE WINS:

Chicago minus-3 at Minnesota This was one of those ABC-TV Thursday night spectaculars, and it got my week off to a good start. I had the tough Bears 6 points better than the so-so Vikings and made a nice bet, even though Bears QB McMahon was supposed to be hurt and Steve Fuller was taking his place. Didn't Fuller get the Bears past Washington in last year's playoffs? Turns out, I was right for the wrong reason. Fuller was lousy and McMahon came in with his team behind and played like Frank Merriwell. Two of his first four passes went for touchdowns. The Bears pulled it out, 33–24.

Indianapolis (0–2) plus-5 at home against Detroit (2–0) The Lions beat Dallas last week, but they are an ordinary team that shouldn't rate more than a 3-point edge against the also ordinary Colts on the road. The Colts, making their 1985 debut before an enthusiastic crowd in the Hoosierdome, played inspired football and won, 14–6.

Philadelphia (0–2) plus-14½ at Washington (1–1)   My figures made this game Washington plus-9. I would have bet heavily, but the presence of Eagles' rookie quarterback Cunningham scared me off. Lo and behold, the defensively tough Eagles won, 19–6. I'm beginning to suspect that the Redskins aren't as good as I thought they were.

San Diego (1–1) plus-5 at Cincinnati (0–2)   This game opened with the Chargers plus-4. I waited until it hit plus-5, and struck. I figured that Chargers' QB Fouts would take advantage of the Bengals' weak cornerbacks. He did, and the Chargers won, 44–41. A typical San Diego offensive game.

Pittsburgh (1–1) minus-5½ at home versus Houston (1–1)   The Steelers had lost the Monday night before to arch-rival Cleveland, making far too many mistakes for a Chuck Noll–coached team. The Oilers looked hot after their win over Miami and near-miss versus Washington. The points on the Steelers dropped to 5½ from 6½ during the week. My numbers had Pittsburgh winning easily. They did, 20–0.

Miami (1–1) plus-4 at home versus Kansas City (2–0)   The Chiefs destroyed the Raiders 36–20, on Thursday night television the week before, and their bandwagon was groaning with passengers. I was impressed, too, but my power-rating numbers, still reflecting last year's differences between the teams, kept me from getting carried away. I made the Dolphins a solid pick at home and Marino, with two games under his belt, made me look good, 31–0. The moral: teams usually don't change all that much from one year to the next.

San Francisco (1–1) minus-2½ at the Los Angeles Raiders (1–1)   This wasn't a strong selection for me. I had the 49ers minus-3½, and they were minus-3 in the opening line. When the points dropped below three—a "key" number—I took a small plunge. The 49ers displayed their Super Bowl form and won, 34-10. To be honest, I was surprised at the size of their margin.

Los Angeles Rams (2-0) plus-7½ at Seattle (2-1) The Seahawks had given up 59 points in winning their first two games, and it was apparent to me that their defense wasn't humming the way it had last year. The Rams didn't wow anyone in beating Denver and Philly, but they did it without Dickerson, and he was due to return versus Seattle. I had the Seahawks favored, but 7½ points on a good running team with a good defense is always a good bet. The Rams won, 35-24.

THE LOSS:

Cleveland (1-1) plus-7½ at Dallas (1-1) I watched the full 60 minutes of this one, and it was a tough loss. Danielson, the Browns' quarterback, called a good game, but made two costly mistakes near the Cowboys' goal line. I'd take the same spread if the two teams played again the next week. But—hey!—with the week I had, I can't complain.

RECORD TO DATE: 11 WINS, 10 LOSSES

WEEK 4

I guess old buddy Lee Pete heard about my 8-1 week, because he asked me back for his Saturday night radio program. Showing that I'm not a superstitious guy, I accepted. Once again, the sharp pencils were poised as I made my selections. Once again, I bombed, with a 2–4 performance. Maybe I ought to start being superstitious.

THE WINS:

Cleveland (1–2) plus-4½ at San Diego (2–1)   I knew that the Browns had a stouter defense than the Chargers, and I thought that would at least keep the score close. They didn't need much defense in this one. San Diego QB Fouts got hurt early and was replaced by Mark Herrmann, who was ineffective. The Chargers averaged 31 points a game their first three outings. They scored 7 this week. Cleveland had 21.

Cincinnati (0–3) plus-6½ at Pittsburgh (2–1)   I shopped and shopped for 7 points but couldn't get it, so I didn't make a very big wager on this Monday night game between conference rivals. The high-scoring Bengals (92 points in the first three weeks) scored high again, and showed some defense for a change. They won it, 37–24.

THE LOSSES:

Washington (1–2) plus-6½ at Chicago (3–0)   Despite the Redskins' shaky start, I thought this was the best bet of the young season. I figured the Redskins would be hot for revenge after being upset by the Bears in the 1984 playoffs. Washington played the first quarter like men possessed and led, 10–0. The Bears ran back the next kickoff to score, and later in the second quarter the Skin's punter got hurt. Quarterback Theismann took his place and punted from deep in his own territory. The punt traveled 62 yards—30 yards up in the air, 30 yards down, and 2 yards out. The writing was on the wall, and so were the Skins' hides. Bears 45, Redskins 10. Ouch.

Green Bay (1-2) plus-8 at St. Louis (2-1)   Veteran Packer QB Dickey, disgusted with his performance in a 24-3 loss to the Jets the week before, benched himself in favor of youngster Randy Wright. I thought that the public had overreacted to that development, and that Wright could hold up his end. He couldn't. The Cards took a big lead and won, 43-28, even though Dickey came in to rally the Packers late.

Tampa Bay (0-3) plus-5 at Detroit (2-1)   I thought that the Bucs were better than their record, and that the Lions were worse than theirs. Wrongo. The Lions won, 30-9.

Buffalo (0-3) plus-3½ at home versus Minnesota (2-1)   I worked hard getting that last half-point, and it almost paid off. The game was tied 20-20 late in the fourth quarter. The Vikings had third down and goal at the Bills' 11 yard line. Did they play it safe and go for a field goal that would have made both them and me happy? Nooooo. Ted Brown took a Statue of Liberty handoff and ran in for the touchdown. Minnesota 27, Buffalo 20.

I saved myself a loss this week by passing the Atlanta-L.A. Rams game. I wanted 10 points on the Falcons and refused to bite on the 9. The Rams won by 11. I took some satisfaction from displaying that discipline.

RECORD TO DATE: 13 WINS, 14 LOSSES

WEEK 5

Betting is funny. Some weeks you have to strain to find anything you like. Some weeks everything looks good. This was one of the latter-type weeks. Believe it or not, I liked 12 games, played them all, and won 10 of them. Eight of my victories were with underdogs. I not only went solidly into the plus side in the won-lost column for the season, but I also got back some of the close games I'd lost earlier in the season. Those things always even out in the long run.

THE WINS:

Pittsburgh (2-2) plus-7½ at Miami (3-1)   This one came under the revenge-factor heading because Miami had beaten the Steelers in the playoffs the season before. I was delighted to get the 7½ points. I thought that the Dolphins' loss to injury of Mark Duper, their super-speedy receiver, would hurt. Pittsburgh hung tough and lost by 4, 24-20.

New England (2-2) plus-4½ at Cleveland (2-2) My patience pays off again. The Browns were a 3½-point favorite most of the week, and I held back. Ten minutes before game time I found the Patriots plus-4 at one bookmaking shop, and plus-4½ at another. I took both. The Browns won, 24-20, so I tied the four and won the 4½. That goes down as a win in my book.

Green Bay (1-3) minus-3½ at home versus Detroit (3-1)   The Packers announced that Dickey would return at quarterback for this game, and I counted that in their favor. My power-rating numbers continued to show that the Lions were worse than their record, and I continued to believe them. The Packers slaughtered them, 43-10.

Philadelphia (1-3) plus-3½ at New Orleans (2-2)   I watched this game on TV and never thought I'd win it. The Saints jumped off to a big lead as Cunningham, the Eagles' rookie QB, foundered. Veteran Ron Jaworski took Cunningham's place in the second half and almost saved the game. At least he saved my bet. The Saints just hung on to win, 23–21.

Tampa Bay (0–4) plus-9 at home versus Chicago (4–0) This game opened at Chicago minus-7½ and closed at minus-9. The Bears won by 8, 27–19, so I (and other people) could have had a middle. The Bucs led by 12 points before collapsing. I considered myself lucky to win this one with a team that was showing numerous shortcomings.

New York Jets (3–1) plus-3 at Cincinnati (1–3) This was a good bet for me. The tough Jets had won three straight games after their opening-game loss to the Raiders. Cincinnati gave up 34 points a game in its first four. I like the Bengals mostly when I get points on them. The Jets won it, 29–20.

San Diego (2–2) plus-13½ at Seattle (2–2) After the first four games of the season, Seattle had given up more points than it had scored. The high-scoring Chargers were hurting, but I figured they could get it up for a divisional foe. I couldn't conceive how the books made this game 13½. The Chargers went down fighting, 26–21.

Denver (2–2) minus-8 at home versus Houston (1–3) I made Denver a 10½-point pick in this one at home against a Houston team that had lost three straight. I would have made a much larger bet if the spread had been 7 points. As it was, I waited until Sunday before betting to make sure that bad weather wouldn't hold down the score. The Broncos won for me, 31–20.

Dallas (4–0) plus-2 at the New York Giants (3–1) This was a Sunday night special on ABC. The bookies' number was within a point of mine, and I would have passed if I'd had a bad or mediocre week, but with their money in my pocket I took a chance on the Cowboys. It was a terrific game, with Dallas winning, 30–29, on a late field goal. When you're hot, you're hot.

Washington (1-3) plus-2 at home versus St. Louis (3-1) I'd just about written off the Redskins as a possible Super Bowl winner, but I figured they'd give a good account of themselves at home against a divisional foe on Monday night. You don't often get the Skins and the points under those circumstances, especially against a team whose defense was proving very leaky (26.5 points per game allowed). Washington won, 27–10.

THE LOSSES:

Buffalo (0-4) plus-4 at Indianapolis (1-3) This was a 3-point game all week. I got my 4 points five minutes before the kickoff at the Stardust. I should have saved my money. The Colts whomped them, 49–17.

Atlanta (0-4) plus-12 at home versus San Francisco (2-2) The 49ers were lucky to beat so-so New Orleans the week before, 20–17. It was beginning to look like another off-year for them after a Super Bowl win. My bet looked good for three quarters, but the Niners came on strong to win, 44–28.

RECORD TO DATE: 23 WINS, 16 LOSSES

WEEK 6

A gambler met a wise man on the Strip. "I can't seem to win two weeks in a row. What should I do?" the gambler asked. "Bet every other week," said the wise man. I should have followed that advice. I went 3–4 after my great fifth week.

THE WINS:

Tampa Bay (0–5) plus-7 at home versus the Los Angeles Rams (5–0) They say that no horse dies a maiden, and few NFL teams go through a season without winning. For all their problems, I figured that the Bucs could stay close to the Rams, who were sluggish offensively despite their five straight wins. They did, losing 31–27.

Atlanta (0–5) plus-14 at Seattle (3–2) The bookmakers who just take a line and post it didn't realize that the Seahawks were averaging 27 points a game while giving up 29 points. Why should they be favored by two touchdowns over anyone? Seattle had to come from behind to win, 30–26.

San Diego (2–3) plus-5 at home versus Kansas City (3–2) I thought that the spread here was too much affected by the Chiefs' impressive wins over New Orleans and the Raiders in their first two games, because they'd been only so-so since. It was a perfect illustration of how a big win on national television, such as the Chiefs' victory over the Raiders, can warp the public's perception of a team for weeks to come. Even without Fouts, San Diego still had punch, and won easily, 31–20.

THE LOSSES:

Pittsburgh (2–3) plus-6 at Dallas (4–1) This is one interconference rivalry that's always been very competitive because of the proud recent histories of the two teams, and the Steelers usually do well against the Cowboys. Dallas won big this time, 27–13, but the game was closer than the score indicates.

Detroit (3–2) plus-10 at Washington (2–3)   As I said before, I didn't think the Lions were much good, but I don't bet on teams, I bet on prices, and the 10 points looked tempting to me. With the divisional rival New York Giants coming up for the Skins the following week, I figured the Lions could keep it close. I was wrong. Washington won, 24–3.

San Francisco (3–2) minus-3½ at home versus Chicago (5–0)   I had the 49ers by 6 in this one, and I bet early when I saw the 3½. Everybody jumped in on San Francisco later in the week and the points climbed as high as 6 before moving back some. If I'd waited until the line settled, as I usually do, I would have passed. Fools rush in, etc. The Bears showed they are for real against anyone this season by whipping the Niners, 26–10.

Buffalo (0–5) plus-10½ at New England (2–3)   I looked all week for 11 points on the Bills and found a little on Saturday, but not enough to offset a larger bet I'd made at 10½. I thought Buffalo could stay close against a Patriot team that was having trouble getting started. It couldn't quite make it, losing 14–3.

RECORD TO DATE: 26 WINS, 20 LOSSES

WEEK 7

I knew this would be an unusual week for me on Saturday, when I did the Lee Pete show again. I boldly predicted that Buffalo and Atlanta, two of the NFL's three remaining winless teams (Tampa Bay was the other), would win their first games on Sunday. Instead of cheers all around, one drunk in the crowd wanted to fight me over that! I still don't know why.

Things got weirder when play started. I won four and lost five for the week, and in four of my losses the teams I'd bet on had their quarterbacks leave the game with illness or injury, or play despite them. Unbelievable! Those things don't reflect negatively on a handicapper's figures, so I just wrote them off to bad luck. But that doesn't make the money loss easier.

THE WINS:

Atlanta (0–6) plus-1 at home versus New Orleans (3–3) My first Winless Wonder comes through. The Falcons are no great shakes, but they were like a cheap claiming horse dropping down in class after getting beat in better company. Final score: Atlanta 31, New Orleans 24.

Buffalo (0–6) plus-1 at home versus Indianapolis (2–4) The Bills had a few players healthy who'd missed the first game between the two teams, and the home field gave them an added boost. Another claiming horse that found its level. Bills 21, Colts 9.

Houston (1–5) plus-4 at home versus Cincinnati (2–4) The Oilers had played pretty well in some of their losses, and the Bengals' defense (almost 33 points per game allowed) wasn't getting any better. It got worse on Sunday. Houston won, 44–27.

Seattle (4–2) plus-4 at Denver (4–2) My power ratings had Denver minus-2 in this one, and the spread all week was the Broncos minus-3. Just as they were teeing up the ball I found my 4 and bet—my "key number" theory in action again. In a good defensive battle, the Broncos won, 13–10, in overtime, and my 4 points stood up.

THE LOSSES:

Dallas (5-1) minus-3½ at Philadelphia (2-4) I made the Cowboys a solid, 7-point favorite in this one, and they were playing like one until quarterback Danny White had to leave with an injury. Gary Hogeboom took over, and his idleness showed when he threw two interceptions in scoring opportunities. The Eagles rallied and won, 16–14, on a deflected-pass touchdown.

San Francisco (3-3) minus-10 at Detroit (3-3) The game opened at 10 and went to 12. I bet early. Just before game time the spread dropped to 9½ after it was announced on a pre-game television show that Montana, the Niners' quarterback, had the flu and might not play. He started, but he should have stood in bed. The Lions won, 23–21.

Los Angeles Raiders (4-2) minus-1½ at Cleveland (4-2) This time it was Raiders' QB Marc Wilson's turn to get hurt. He played with bruised ribs, but not well. The Raiders skinned by, 21–20. I lost by a lousy one-half point.

Miami (4-2) minus-13 at home versus Tampa Bay (0-6) I very seldom lay 13 points on an NFL game, but Miami was a solid 16-point choice here in my book. The Dolphins had looked bad losing to the Jets in New York the week before, and I expected them to bounce back strong at home against their in-state rival. They had a 17-point lead and the ball in the second half when a fumble recovery woke up the Bucs. Miami had to kick a late field goal to win, 41–38.

Green Bay (3-3) plus-10 at Chicago (6-0) I lost Packer quarterback Dickey to injury during this Monday night game. More important, Bears' coach Ditka outsmarted and humiliated the Packers by putting William "The Refrigerator" Perry, a 308-pound rookie defensive lineman, into the game as a back in goal-line situations. Perry threw a terrific block on one short-yardage touchdown run, and carried the ball in himself for another. The Bears won, 23-7, and were trying to rub it in further by passing for more points as the game ended. I marked down a revenge-factor bet on the Packers for the next time the two old rivals met.

RECORD TO DATE: 30 WINS, 25 LOSSES

WEEK 8

One of the more important things I look for in NFL games beginning around mid-season is a situation where an above-average team *must win* a game in order to stay in contention for a playoff spot. Teams don't always come through in those spots, but you're always assured of a good effort. I found two teams on the must-win list this week, and they helped me to a 4-1 mark.

THE WINS:

Washington (3-4) plus-3 at Cleveland (4-3) This was a do-or-die spot for the Redskins, who were tied for third in the NFC East, two full games behind Dallas. They'd been beaten by the Giants the week before, and another loss might have killed them. I liked them in this game because they had more experience in the skilled positions than the Browns, who were starting rookie Bernie Kosar at quarterback in place of Gary Danielson. Washington won it, 14-7, thanks in part to some shaky work by Kosar.

San Francisco (3–4) plus-1 at the Los Angeles Rams (7–0)   The defending Super Bowl champs were up against it even worse than the Redskins. A loss to the unbeaten Rams would have killed their shot at a division title and about flushed their wild-card hopes as well. Montana was out of his sickbed and ready to rumble. All the signs looked favorable, so I made a *giant* wager here. The Niners won, 28–14, and so did I.

Chicago (7–0) minus-7 at home versus Minnesota (4–3)   I had the Bears 9 points better than the Vikings in this one. They were clearly the superior team and I couldn't see how they could lose straight up, especially at home. The 7-point spread in this one looked like money in the bank. Sure enough, the Bears prevailed, 27–9.

Buffalo (1–6) plus-10 at Philadelphia (3–4)   Yeah, Buffalo was lousy, but the 10 points looked very good against an Eagles team that had been scoring only 14 points a game. Philadelphia had to come from behind to win, 21–17.

THE LOSS:

Atlanta (1–6) plus-13½ at Dallas (5–2)   Another case where the points seemed to justify the bet, especially with the Cowboys facing road games against divisional rivals St. Louis and Washington the following two weeks. The Cowboys won, 24–10, with Falcon kicker Mick Luckhurst missing a 27-yard chip-shot field goal try. A half-point loss for me.

RECORD TO DATE: 34 WINS, 26 LOSSES

WEEK 9

I went 4–3 this week, and I wasn't feeling too good about it until I got out my calculator and figured that four wins in seven games all season long would give me 57 percent wins. Any handicapper would be proud to show that sort of mark over the long haul. That made me feel better. So did the fact that I won my biggest bet of the week—my revenge-factor pick of the Packers against the Bears.

THE WINS:

Green Bay (3–5) plus-9 at home versus Chicago (8–0)   It was take-no-prisoners day at Lambeau Field. In one of the nastiest, dirtiest games I can remember, the Packers went all out to avenge their Monday night loss of two weeks before. The Bears won, 16–10, behind Walter Payton's running, but not without a terrific struggle. Chicago did get in one good lick, though. "Refrigerator" Perry caught a pass for a touchdown! A nice win for me.

Tampa Bay (0–8) plus 12½ at the New York Giants (5–3)   Las Vegas doesn't have a home team in the NFL, but four teams always get a heavy play here. They are the Giants and Jets, because of all the transplanted New Yorkers in town, and the Rams and Raiders, because of the weekend tourists from L.A. I could think of no other reasons for the tough but low-scoring Giants to be a 12½-point pick here. "The Giants never cover as a favorite. Who are they to be minus-12½?" asked my friend Moe, a former Easterner. I asked him if he was taking the Bucs. "Nah. I don't like either team," he said. Typical. The Giants just skinned through, 22–20.

Seattle (4–4) minus-1 at home versus the Los Angeles Raiders (6–2)   This wasn't a strong pick for me. The Seahawks had lost two in a row (to Denver and the

Jets), and weren't scoring. Still, they were at home and in a must-win situation against a Raider team that looked a little soft after winning five straight. Chuck Knox's team surprised me with a lopsided, 33–3, victory.

St. Louis (3–5) plus-4½ at home versus Dallas (6–2) This was another game that appealed to my contrary nature. The Cards, a lot of people's preseason Super Bowl pick, obviously weren't a top team, and they were playing without their best runner, O. J. Anderson, and best receiver, Roy Green. But it was Monday night and they were at home against the hated Cowboys. In an emotional game, the Cards came out on top, 21–10.

THE LOSSES:

Buffalo (1–7) plus-4 at home against Cincinnati (3–5) Another bet against the leaky Bengals, who had given up 32.6 points a game on the season while scoring 29.6. I was looking good as the Bills jumped off to their usual early lead, but again they faded late to lose, 23–17. If the games were 50 minutes long, the Bills would be contenders.

Atlanta (1–7) plus-6½ at home versus Washington (4–4) The Falcons had beaten New Orleans and looked decent in losing to Dallas in the two games before this one. The Redskins had arch-rival Dallas on their schedule for the following week. I tried to steal one here, but couldn't. Washington 44, Atlanta 10.

Philadelphia (4–4) plus-10 at San Francisco (4–4) This was basically a bet on a Philadelphia team that had won three straight (versus St. Louis, Dallas, and Buffalo) and had the fourth-best points-allowed mark in the NFL at 15.1 a game. The 49ers won, 24–13, but it was a tough battle and the Eagles wasted three late-scoring chances.

RECORD TO DATE: 38 WINS, 29 LOSSES

WEEK 10

This week's games provided a couple of good examples of the public overreacting to injuries to quarterbacks. I jumped on the other side of both of them and won nice bets. They helped me to a 6–2–1 week.

THE WINS:

Los Angeles Rams (8–1) plus-5½ at the New York Giants (6–3) The Giants opened minus-3½ here. Then word got out that the Rams were going with Jeff Kemp, their second-string quarterback, because of an injury to Dieter Brock, their starter, and the spread jumped to 5 and 5½. I thought the Rams would do very well with Kemp. He was their starter last season, and knew their system and players. As I have mentioned before, 5 and 5½ points usually are dead numbers, but they lived in New York on this Sunday. The Giants won, 24–19, and I got a half-point win.

Chicago (9–0) minus-9 at home versus Detroit (5–4) This situation was about identical to the Rams-Giants one. The game opened Chicago minus-11, but the story broke that Bears' quarterback McMahon had a bad shoulder, and that second-stringer Steve Fuller would play instead. The Bears dropped to minus-9. Like Kemp, Fuller was a seasoned player who had seen a lot of action the year before. I didn't think the Bears could win the Super Bowl with him, but he seemed more than good enough to handle the mediocre Lions at home in front of a big TV audience on CBS. The Bears dominated, 24–3.

Pittsburgh (4–5) plus-2 at Kansas City (3–6)   This wasn't a hard selection to make. Kansas City had lost five straight and stories were circulating about dissension on the team. Pittsburgh wasn't showing a lot of zip, but they were playing their games in typical, tough Steeler fashion and looked good as an underdog. Pittsburgh won, 36–28.

San Diego (4–5) plus-3 at home versus the Los Angeles Raiders (6–3)   The Chargers were healthier than they'd been all season, and I liked their prospects of getting points on the board versus the Raiders, whose defense had slipped from their 1984 Super Bowl year. I waited for 3 points and got them at two places just before game time. The Chargers won it, 40–34, in an exciting game that went into overtime.

Dallas (6–3) plus-3 at Washington (5–4)   Dallas destroyed the Skins, 44–14, on opening day, and a lot of people tabbed this as a strong revenge-factor play on Washington. I didn't, because *the revenge factor works best when you have the superior team or are getting points.* I made the Cowboys the favorite in this game, and placed my biggest bet of the day when I got the 3 points. Dallas controlled the play throughout and won, 13–7.

Denver (6–3) plus-3½ at home versus San Francisco (5–4)   The 49ers had won two straight and people were starting to think they were back to their Super Bowl form of the previous season. I looked at the other side: a Denver team with a better won-lost record, playing at home where they're always tough, on Monday night television, and *with* 3½ points. I jumped in on the Broncos, and they won it, 17–16, on a late field goal.

THE LOSSES:

New Orleans (3-6) plus-6½ at home versus Seattle (5-4)   What can I say about this one? I figured that the Seahawks would look on the game as a breather between two tough foes, the Raiders and New England. They didn't, and won, 27–3. The loss made the Saints 2–8 against the spread this season, the worst record in the NFL.

Indianapolis (3-6) plus-10 at New England (6-3)   I thought that the Colts' running game would keep them close against New England, and the 10 points at the Stardust early in the week looked attractive. The Pats, with a revived Steve Grogan calling the shots at quarterback, made me look bad with a 34–15 victory. It was their fifth straight win, and they're starting to look like a contender.

THE TIE:

New York Jets (7-2) plus-4 at Miami (5-4)   Four points were hard to get on this game, but I shopped, and waited, and got them. They saved me a loss. It was a terrific game, with the tough-at-home Dolphins scoring the winning touchdown with less than a minute left. The score was 21–17. I can't overemphasize the importance of shopping for the best available line.

RECORD TO DATE: 44 WINS, 31 LOSSES, 1 TIE

WEEK 11

I've got to hand it to the officials in the NFL. Sure, they make mistakes, but we all do. The difference is that theirs are pointed out on TV, coast to coast, in slow-motion instant replay. I don't think many of us could stand that kind of scrutiny.

What really tickles me is when one of those world-class sprinters who are wide receivers in the league sets off down the sideline on a "fly" pattern, and a 50-year-old official, his whistle in his mouth, is keeping up with him, running backward. After the play, the wide receiver goes to the bench for oxygen, and the official trots back for the next play.

I've got to think amusing thoughts this week because I went 3–5 last weekend, and my biggest bets lost. I don't think I deserved two of my losses, but that's the breaks. The bad news follows.

THE WINS:

Philadelphia (5–5) plus-3 at St. Louis (4–6)   No mystery here. The Eagles were playing solid football, and the Cardinals were beat up all around. They'd given Tampa Bay its first victory of the season the week before. The Eagles won routinely, 24–14.

New England (7–3) plus-5 at Seattle (6–4)   I thought the surging Patriots would keep this one close or win, but I held off making a really large bet because I didn't get the 6 points I was looking for. I should have been braver, because the Pats made it six straight, 20–13.

New York Giants (7–3) at Washington (5–5), over-37   I bet a rare (for me) "over" on this one and won it. My reasoning was that the Skins would go to the air against the Giants' tough defense against the run. They figured to score that way, and their passes would leave more time on the clock for New York to put points on the board. This was the game in which Joe Theismann, the Redskins' quarterback, broke his leg. But with backup Ricky Schroeder at QB, the Skins stuck with the pass and won, 23–21.

THE LOSSES:

Indianapolis (3–7) plus-9 at home versus Miami (6–4) I really liked this game; my figures made the Dolphins a favorite by less than a touchdown. Miami was coming off a tough win against the Jets and figured to have a letdown in the Hoosierdome against a team that's a lot better at home than on the road. I was feeling very comfortable when the Colts took a 10-point first-half lead. The Dolphins caught and passed them, but I was alive until the last couple of minutes or so, when an official ruled incomplete a Colt pass to the Dolphins' 2-yard line that the replay showed was caught. I take back whatever nice things I said about the refs. Miami 34, Colts 20.

Cincinnati (5–5) plus-6½ at the Los Angeles Raiders (6–4) Another heartbreaker. I wanted 7 points on this game, but was lucky to get the 6½ because the line dropped to 5½ in some places by week's end. The Bengals had won three straight, were healthy, and usually make a good underdog. They played their best defensive game of the season in this one. It was tied, 6–6, late in the fourth quarter. The Raiders had a third-and-three deep in Bengals' territory with a sure field goal in prospect. Instead of a safe handoff, they passed for a touchdown that won it, 13–6.

New Orleans (3–7) plus-9 versus Green Bay (4–6) at Milwaukee Yeah, I know what I said about the Saints, but this was supposed to be a must-win game for "Bum" Phillips, their popular coach, and the Packers were a so-so team. I watched the game, and Phillips deserves to be fired. I never saw a team so poorly prepared. The Packers romped, 38–14.

Minnesota (5–5) plus-3½ at Detroit (5–5) The extra half-point hooked me in this game between conference rivals. Minnesota had a very good history against the Lions, and looked to have enough variety in their offense to win against an in-and-out Detroit team. But the Vikings made four first-quarter turnovers and were blown out, 41–21.

Kansas City (3–7) plus-12½ at San Francisco (5–5) This was a classic good team–bad team matchup. As usual, I took the bad team—with the points. It would have taken 28½ points for me to win this one. San Francisco 31, Chiefs 3.

RECORD TO DATE: 47 WINS, 36 LOSSES, 1 TIE

WEEK 12

If you can't get a half-point you want, and all your shopping fails, you can buy it by laying 6 to 5 odds on a game instead of the usual 11 to 10, or 5½ to 5. I do this very seldom, because betting into the 6 to 5 often is a recipe for disaster. But I did it this week to good effect in the Buffalo-Miami game. I would have won the game anyway because of a missed extra point, but that's not something you can figure beforehand. In all, I went 3–3–1 for the week.

THE WINS:

***Buffalo (2–9) plus-10 at home versus Miami
(7–4)*** I bought the half-point at Caesars Palace. The Bills
were changing to young Bruce Mathison at quarterback,
and I figured the move could only help this going-nowhere
team. Buffalo was playing decent defense and had the
home field. Miami promised to be diverted by the prospect
of playing the mighty Bears at home the following week. It
turned out that it took a missed extra point to give me the
win in a 23–14 Miami victory. Whew!

***Houston (4–7) plus-7 at home versus San Diego
(5–6)*** This was the most ridiculous price of the week. The
Chargers opened at minus-4½ and closed at minus-6½ or
minus-7 points in most books. They had Dan Fouts
healthy again at quarterback and were scoring points by
the bushel. But their defense remained terrible and Houston, with Moon at quarterback, had some punch. In a see-
saw battle that featured three scores in the final two
minutes, the Oilers won, 37–35.

***Denver (8–3) plus-6 at the Los Angeles Raiders
(7–4)*** The Raiders usually are overpriced in Las Vegas
because of the Route-15 crowd, and this game was no exception. I had L.A. only a 3-point pick, and made a nice-
sized bet. Bronco quarterback Elway avoided the Raider
blitzes with rollouts, and kept his team in the game. The
Raiders won in overtime, 31–28.

THE LOSSES:

Atlanta (2–9) plus-16 1/2 at Chicago (11–0) It's
hard for me to pass up 16½ points on an NFL game. I
hoped the Bears would be looking past Atlanta to Miami
the following week, and the weather in Soldier Field in

Chicago on the November 24 game day promised to be cold enough to hold down the score. No such luck. The Bears whomped 'em, 36–0, with The Refrigerator scoring again. The cold doesn't bother him.

Green Bay (5–6) plus-6½ at the Los Angeles Rams (8–3)   The Packers had scored 65 points in winning their last two outings, and I was counting on their offense to stay hot against a Rams team that had lost two straight and three of four. The Rams returned the opening kickoff for a touchdown, and there went my 6½ points. They prevailed by a comfortable, 34–17.

Philadelphia (6–5) plus-7½ at Dallas (7–4)   The Cowboys had two psychological factors going for them: the desire to rebound from their 44–0 home humiliation by the Bears the week before, and revenge for their 16–14 loss to the Eagles earlier. I thought those were overbalanced by the tough Eagle defense and those big 7½ points. It turned out to be a surprisingly high-scoring game. The Eagles moved the ball well, but some key penalties hurt them. Dallas won, 34–17.

THE TIE:

New York Jets (8–3) minus-3 at home versus New England (8–3)   This game was 4 and 3½ points all week. I held out for the 3 until the end, and got it. The result was another tie where I could have had a loss. The Jets won in overtime, 16–13.

RECORD TO DATE: 50 WINS, 39 LOSSES, 2 TIES

WEEK 13

Arf! Arf! The dogs were really barking this week. I took eight of them in my nine selections. I went 4-4-1 in the won-lost column for my second straight sister-kisser. I wasn't too unhappy, though, because I cashed my biggest bet of the season on Miami against the Bears on Monday night.

THE WINS:

Miami (8-4) plus-4 at home versus Chicago (12-0) The Bears went into this one unbeaten. They'd also scored more points than any NFL team, and allowed fewest. But I thought that the Dolphins had a decided edge. They were playing for first place in their division while the Bears had theirs clinched. They were at home in the Orange Bowl, where they rarely lose. And the Bears were starting backup quarterback Fuller against the Dolphins' first-stringer, Marino.

As I said earlier, Fuller was good enough to beat the likes of the Lions, but this was the Dolphins. I liked this game so much that in addition to a large bet at 11 to 10 odds with the points I also took the Fins to win straight up at 8 to 5 odds in my favor. That's an unusual bet for me. If you saw the game—and you probably did because it drew the biggest Monday night TV audience ever—you saw a superb Miami passing attack take the Bears apart, 38-24.

Minnesota (5-7) plus-7½ at Philadelphia (6-6) I love to go against injury-inflated prices, and this was one. The Eagles opened minus-6, and the line jumped to 7½ on news that Viking QB Tommy Kramer wouldn't play. I thought that his backup, Wade Wilson, a 5-year vet, wasn't that much worse. It was a weird game. The Eagles led, 23-0 in the fourth quarter. Then the Vikings scored four touchdowns in the final 8 minutes to win, 28-23.

New Orleans (4–8) plus-7 at home versus the Los Angeles Rams (9–3) "Bum" Phillips was out as the Saints' coach and his son, Wade, had the job for the rest of the season. I figured that had to be good. I wanted at least 7 points, and got them just before kickoff. The Rams had sleepwalked to a loss at Atlanta two weeks earlier. They did it again in the Superdome, losing 29–3.

San Francisco (7–5) minus-4 at Washington (7–5) The same point about backup quarterbacks that helped me pick Miami this week led me to this choice. The Redskins' Schroeder had led his team to wins over the Giants and Steelers, but I figured that the revived 49ers would be a different proposition altogether. The San Francisco defense chased Schroeder all over the field with blitzes, and the 49er offense rolled. Final score: 35–8.

THE LOSSES:

St. Louis (4–8) plus-14½ at Dallas (8–4) on Thanksgiving Day I lost this bet but wasn't sorry I'd made it. With Roy Green, the Cards' best receiver, back in the starting lineup, 14½ points looked awfully good in a clash between NFC Eastern Division rivals. It was a fairly close game until Cowboys' quarterback White began exploiting a weakness on the right side of the Cards' defensive backfield in the second half. Even so, I was in it until the end, when a St. Louis drive died on the Dallas 6-yard line. The Cowboys won, 35–17.

Houston (5–7) plus-9 at Cincinnati (5–7) The season was three-fourths over and the Bengals were still giving up more points than they were scoring. Some 9-point favorite! Their defense was terrible again here, but their offense was terrific. Bengals 45, Oilers 27.

Buffalo (2–10) plus-11 at San Diego (5–7)   No point rehashing a game in which my team was demolished, 40–7, but it proved an interesting point. Despite the lopsided final score, the yardage statistics wound up almost equal in all departments. It just goes to show how misleading statistics can be.

Atlanta (2–10) plus-8 at home versus the Los Angeles Raiders (8–4)   I had the game Raiders minus-6, and I took Atlanta even though they looked like the weaker team. I watched on TV as Atlanta grabbed a 17–13 halftime edge despite an obvious disadvantage along the line of scrimmage. I called some bookies and found out that the Raiders were a 6½-point favorite in the second half. I gave the points on that one, washing out my original bet. I didn't discuss halftime betting in my money-management chapter because you can't get that kind of wager in many places outside Las Vegas. In this game, L.A. dominated the second half, 21–7, and won the game, 34–24. I finished about even in the money department on this one, but I'll still take the loss for scorekeeping purposes.

THE TIE:

Indianapolis (3–9) plus-7 at home versus New England (8–4)   The Colts had won four of five at home against the spread, and, as I mentioned before, could have been five of five if not for an official's bad call against Miami. Another bad call on a pass to the Pats' Stanley Morgan (it was ruled a touchdown even though the replay showed he was out of bounds) hurt them in this one, a 38–31 New England victory.

RECORD TO DATE: 54 WINS, 43 LOSSES, 3 TIES

WEEK 14

THE WINS:

I made my biggest halftime bet of the season on Sunday, and I won it. It helped me to a 4–3 week. I made it on the L.A. Raiders. They were a 3-point underdog at Denver with first place in the AFC West on the line. I also made the game Denver minus-3, so I passed it initially. But when the Broncos took a 14–0 halftime lead, I took the Raiders minus-3½ in the second half. It was a classic halftime bet because I was getting an outstanding team with a good scoring average (24 points a game) taking a shutout into the second half of a must-win contest. Good teams that are trailing usually are favored in halftime bets, but this one looked too good to pass. And true to form, the Raiders got untracked after intermission and wound up beating the Broncos in overtime, 17–14.

I make lots of halftime wagers during a season, but usually they're small and intended to try to correct mistakes I make in my initial bets on games. I include this one in my season won-lost total because it was as large as my usual bets, and my only one on that game.

Indianapolis (3–10) plus-20 at Chicago (12–1)
The Bears had lost their bid for an undefeated season the weekend before, but they'd still clinched their division title and the home field through the NFC playoffs. They came out of the Miami contest down mentally, and Walter Payton, their great running back, had the flu during the week. Twenty points were hard to pass up on a young Colts team that figured to be trying hard before a rare (for them) national television audience on CBS. The Bears played conservatively and won, 17–10.

St. Louis (4–9) minus-3 at home versus New Orleans (5–8) The Cardinals were having a poor season, but they'd played decently losing to Dallas on Thanksgiving the week before, and had a 10-day break before this game. I thought they had more sock than the so-so Saints. They did, 28–16.

Los Angeles Rams (9–4) plus-10 at San Francisco (8–5) The Rams had lost three of four going into this one, and their once large lead in the NFC West as well as their playoff hopes were dwindling. I looked for them to make a big effort against their in-state rival. I made a good-sized bet on them with the 10 points, and another when a bookmaker offered me 11 to 5 odds if I'd take the Rams plus-4½. The game was a tough one, with turnovers playing a big role. A runback of a tipped-pass interception gave the Rams a 27–20 victory and me a two-bet win.

THE LOSSES:

Philadelphia (6–7) plus-1 at home versus Washington (7–6) I really liked the Eagles in this one. Veteran Ron Jaworski was going well again at quarterback for them, and I thought he was clearly better than the Redskins' Schroeder. The Eagles were at home, and I thought my 1-point edge might very well come into play in what promised to be a close, low-scoring game. It was close and low scoring, all right, but the Skins prevailed, 17–12.

Buffalo (2–11) plus-10 at home against the New York Jets (9–4) I would have passed this one if I hadn't gotten the 10 points. Too bad for me that I did. I figured that the Bills would be able to stay close to a Jets team playing with three starting defensive backs out with injuries. I didn't watch, but the papers said the pathetic Bills came up empty four times inside the Jets' 10-yard line. New York won, 27–7.

Pittsburgh (6–7) plus-6 at San Diego (6–7)   The Steelers needed to win this one to stay in the playoff picture in the close AFC Central Division against a high-scoring, poor-defense Chargers team that was playing out the string. The game was a lot wilder than I thought it would be, but I was feeling good when my wife called me to dinner with Pittsburgh ahead by 3 points and just over 2 minutes left. I kept the TV on in the next room and heard the Chargers score a touchdown and miss the extra point to take a 3-point lead. I was still listening when they ran back an intercepted Steeler pass to finish off a 54–44 win. I forget what I had for dinner, but I remember the indigestion.

RECORD TO DATE: 58 WINS, 46 LOSSES, 3 TIES

WEEK 15

It is Tuesday, December 17, and that song from the musical *Oklahoma* is running through my head, the one that goes "Oh, What a Beautiful Morning." Hammerstein wrote those lyrics—Oscar, not Mike. After starting the weekend with a Saturday loss on the Bears-Jets game, I came back to win six in a row, including two juicy double wins on full-game and halftime bets. That's enough to make Scrooge jolly.

THE WINS:

Philadelphia (6–8) plus-8 at San Diego (7–7)   Inconsistent San Diego was coming off big victories over Pittsburgh and Houston, while Philadelphia had lost three straight. Norman Braman, the Eagles' owner, was steaming publicly about his team, and I figured it was Survival Bowl time for the Eagles' players. Under those circumstances, the 8 points looked very good. Both teams ate up a lot of real estate in the first half, with the Eagles taking a 7–3 lead. I called a few bookies and learned that the Chargers were 6-point favorites in the second half. I gave the 6 and sat back to watch, fingers crossed. The Chargers charged back to take a 20–14 lead. They had the ball on the Eagles' 6-yard line as time was running out. Instead of going for a touchdown or field goal, they sat on the ball, bless them. I collected on both my game and halftime bets, but I'll count them as one win for my won-lost mark.

Green Bay (6–8) plus-6½ at Detroit (7–7)   I don't know why this meaningless game went from 4½ to 6½ points on the Lions; maybe it was because of their 6–0 home-field record. I thought anything over a field goal was worth taking. That drew some lip from a few of my followers, but most of them had the good sense to keep any mutinous thoughts to themselves. The Lions took a 14–0 lead, but the Packers hung in there and won it, 26–23.

Dallas (9–5) minus-2½ at home versus the New York Giants (9–5)   This was the big game of the season in the NFC East, with the division title and a sure playoff spot on the line. In games like these I like to go with the team that's been on top longer if the points aren't prohibitive. I figured that the veteran Cowboys, playing at home, could handle the Giants, even if the Cowboys weren't the team they used to be. The Giants outgained Dallas, and probably deserved to win, but two quick Cowboy touchdowns at the end of the first half turned it. One came on a long runback of a deflected pass that was intercepted by a lineman. The other came after the Giants' punter couldn't handle the snap from center deep in his own end. The

Cowboys had to hold off a late Giants' rally, but they won, 28–21.

Los Angeles Raiders (10–4) minus-4 at home versus Seattle (8–6) The Raiders could clinch another AFC West title with a win here, while the Seahawks were finishing off a very disappointing season. The Raiders had been slipping by opponents, winning by a field goal here and a touchdown there, but I gave them an edge for superior motivation, home field, and a better offense. The Raiders' pass rush dominated play in a low-scoring game. A late touchdown iced their 13–3 victory.

Atlanta (2–12) plus-2½ at home versus Minnesota (7–7) Another game involving two teams going nowhere. I figured the Falcons might get it up to save the job of Dan Henning, their popular coach. I must admit that I lucked out. Jan Stenerud, the Vikings' 19-year veteran place kicker, missed three field goals (two were blocked) and an extra point. It was enough to persuade him to announce his retirement at the end of this season. Atlanta eked one out for me and Coach Dan, 14–13.

New England (10–4) plus-7 at Miami (10–4) It seemed like all Las Vegas was waiting for the Dolphins to go from their opening price of minus- 6½ to a full 7 points. It happened the afternoon before the Monday night game. This was a must-win situation for two teams battling for the lead in the AFC East. I knew that the Patriots hadn't won in Miami since 1966, but I thought they had better offensive balance and a shade tougher defense than the Dolphins. Miami took a 17–7 halftime lead, and the bookmakers put up a pick-'em price for the second half. I took the Patriots there, too. They came back in the second half and fell just short, 30–27. For the second time in a weekend, I cashed two good-sized bets on the same game, although, again, I'll count it as one win for my season's record.

THE LOSS:

New York Jets (10–4) plus-3 at home versus Chicago (13–1) Trying to get 3 points on the Jets was like trying to find a $20 hooker on the Strip. I didn't look for the hooker, but it would have been cheaper. The Jets' coach, Joe Walton, went down as my boob of the year for his handling of his team. He was down by 7 points in the third quarter with a strong wind at his back, and he ran the ball. In the fourth quarter, into the teeth of the gale, he passed. The Bears, on the road, had everything clinched while the Jets were fighting for a division title and playoff berth. The Bears won anyway, 19–6.

RECORD TO DATE: 64 WINS, 47 LOSSES, 3 TIES

WEEK 16

This was the final week of the regular season and, as usual, some teams jumped out at the bettors because they had to win their games to keep playoff hopes alive or secure homefield advantages in the Super Bowl tournament. There were eight teams in those situations—Denver, the Giants, the Jets, Washington, Miami, New England, San Francisco, and the Raiders—and all of them not only won their games but also covered inflated point spreads. It's always tempting to go with must-win teams in the last week or two of a season, but from my years of gambling I know that it's usually not healthy financially. It's the sort of "system" play that keeps the bookies in Cadillacs and their girlfriends in hair coloring.

As it was, I went 4–3 for the week, to finish the regular season with 68 wins, 50 losses, and 3 ties. That works out to 57.6 percent winners heading into the playoffs. I've done better, but I can't complain, especially since most of my important money bets came through. Here's the rundown on the week.

THE WINS:

New York Jets (10–5) minus-7½ at home versus Cleveland (8–7) This was one must-win team that I took. The Browns had absolutely nothing to gain in this game, having clinched the AFC Central division title the week before. They had a week's vacation ahead of them before the playoffs and would be looking mostly to come out of the game healthy. Denver had beaten Seattle the Friday night before to finish at 11–5, so the Jets had to win to make the playoffs as a wild-card team. They did, 37–10.

New York Giants (9–6) minus-8½ at home versus Pittsburgh (7–8) Another game in which a must-win team faced one that had nothing at stake. I might have skipped this game if the Steelers had shown more fire in their last few outings, but they had sagged badly, losing three straight before edging weak Buffalo by less than a touchdown. Their "down" mentality was unusual for a Chuck Noll–coached team, and I'm sure he'll make some changes before next season. The Steelers went through the motions again here, and the Giants won, 28–10.

Kansas City (5–10) minus-1½ at home versus San Diego (8–7) The Chiefs had turned in strong performances against Denver (a 14–13 loss) and Atlanta (38–10) in their last two games, and I thought they looked like a good bet at home in this "nothing" contest, especially since Dan Fouts was out again for the Chargers. K.C. took a huge lead and barely held on to win, 38–34. Count me lucky.

Los Angeles Raiders (11–4) minus-3 at the Los Angeles Rams (11–4)   This was my biggest bet of the day. The Raiders needed a win to clinch the home field throughout the AFC playoffs. Also, as many Raider fans as Ram fans figured to be at this game, canceling the Rams' home edge. It was a dull, defense-oriented contest, but the Raiders' superior pass rush and more balanced offense prevailed, 16–6, as I thought they would.

THE LOSSES:

St. Louis (5–10) plus-7 at home versus Washington (9–6)   I went against the must-win team here because the Cardinals were healthy and figured to be "up" emotionally against their division rival. Also, Jim Hanifan, the Cards' popular coach, had his neck on the block, and a win might give him a reprieve. The Cards jumped off to an early lead and my bets looked good with inexperienced quarterback Ricky Schroeder at the Redskins' controls. After the Cards had scored to take a 9–0 edge, though, they unwisely tried an onside kickoff that failed. The Skins marched right in for a touchdown and controlled the game thereafter. They won, 27–16, but still didn't make the playoffs because the Giants and 49ers also won.

Detroit (7–8) plus-7½ at home versus Chicago (14–1)   The Bears had sewed up their conference title and home field for the playoffs, and figured to be resting some hurt players. The Lions had a good home record (6–1) and no love for the Bears. This turned out to be a wild game for a season-ender with nothing at stake. The Bears won, 37–17, thanks partly to some officials' questionable calls that went their way.

Houston (5-10) plus-6 at Indianapolis (4-11)
This game opened plus-4 on the Oilers and I got involved
when it went to 6. I had the Colts as no more than a field
goal better. A couple of second-half interceptions stopped
Oilers' drives and left the Colts a 34-16 winner.

RECORD FOR THE REGULAR SEASON: 68-50-3, OR 57.6 PER-
CENT

1985 FINAL STANDINGS
NATIONAL FOOTBALL CONFERENCE

Eastern Division

	W	L	T	Pct.	Pts.	OP
* Dallas	10	6	0	.625	357	333
† New York	10	6	0	.625	399	283
Washington	10	6	0	.625	297	312
Philadelphia	7	9	0	.438	286	310
St. Louis	5	11	0	.313	278	414

Central Division

	W	L	T	Pct.	Pts.	OP
* Chicago	15	1	0	.938	456	198
Green Bay	8	8	0	.500	337	355
Minnesota	7	9	0	.438	346	359
Detroit	7	9	0	.438	307	366
Tampa Bay	2	14	0	.125	294	448

Western Division

	W	L	T	Pct.	Pts.	OP
* L.A. Rams	11	5	0	.688	340	277
† San Francisco	10	6	0	.625	411	263
New Orleans	5	11	0	.313	294	401
Atlanta	4	12	0	.250	282	452

* *Conference champion*   † *Wild-card playoff team*

1985 FINAL STANDINGS
AMERICAN FOOTBALL CONFERENCE

Eastern Division

	W	L	T	Pct.	Pts.	OP
* Miami	12	4	0	.750	428	320
† N.Y. Jets	11	5	0	.688	393	264
† New England	11	5	0	.688	362	290
Indianapolis	5	11	0	.313	320	386
Buffalo	2	14	0	.125	200	381

Central Division

	W	L	T	Pct.	Pts.	OP
* Cleveland	8	8	0	.500	287	294
Cincinnati	7	9	0	.438	441	437
Pittsburgh	7	9	0	.438	379	355
Houston	5	11	0	.313	284	412

Western Division

	W	L	T	Pct.	Pts.	OP
* L.A. Raiders	12	4	0	.750	354	308
Denver	11	5	0	.688	380	329
Seattle	8	8	0	.500	349	303
San Diego	8	8	0	.500	467	435
Kansas City	6	10	0	.376	317	360

* Conference champion   † Wild-card playoff team

THE PLAYOFFS

The NFL playoffs usually present bettors with some problems. There are only two or three games a weekend to bet on instead of the usual 14, and only one game on Super Bowl Sunday. The temptation is great to throw caution to the winds and bet on every game whether or not your opinion justifies it. That's true whether you're ahead or behind financially for the season.

I confess that I usually bet on every playoff game. By the time the playoffs roll around, I've reached some strong conclusions about the contestants, and I'm usually anxious to test them. Betting on every playoff game has made me look good on occasion. I went 9–0 on them in 1981 when I was doing betting columns for several newspapers. How sweet it was, and in public, too! In addition, as I've already mentioned a couple of times, I go into 1986 having bet right on 13 straight Super Bowl games.

WEEK 1

I split the two games on wild-card weekend. My win was on *New England plus-3½ at the New York Jets.* To be perfectly honest, I had no strong opinion on this game, and with the Jets a 3-point pick all over town during the week I was ready to pass on it. But when two of my runners dug up the 3½ points on New England, I took a small plunge.

I thought the Jets rated a slight edge with a healthy Freeman McNeil carrying the ball for them on their home field. On the other side, the offensively balanced Patriots had covered the spread for 11 games in a row. What convinced me to back New England was my opinion of Jets' coach Joe Walton. His performance against the Bears in the wind a couple of weeks before was about the dumbest thing I'd seen all season. I figured that he'd find a way to lose this one if the Patriots gave him any excuse at all. The game was close until the third quarter, when the Pats got some scores on turnovers. They won it handily, 26–14.

I lost the second half of the weekend doubleheader at Giants Stadium in East Rutherford, New Jersey. I took *San Francisco minus-2½ against the home team New York Giants.*

This was another bet that I could have just as well passed up. My numbers had the game dead even, but my heart favored the 49ers off their big win over the Dallas Cowboys the weekend before. I knew that the Niners had been up and down all season, but I thought that the talent was there for another Super Bowl run, and that their win over the Cowboys was the sign that they'd finally got their act together. I put my money down and crossed my fingers.

Five minutes after the CBS-TV pre-game show went on, I knew I was a loser. John Madden said that 49er quarterback Montana was a doubtful starter because of bruised ribs. That was about the best-kept secret of the season! If I'd known about Montana's condition, I would have remained neutral.

Montana wasn't the only walking wounded on the field for the Niners that day. Running back Roger Craig wasn't up to par and Ronnie Lott, their best defensive back, was playing with a little finger that was so badly hurt that he couldn't tackle with his whole arm. The Giants totally dominated the game and won, 17–3. No undefeated playoff season for me this year.

WEEK 2

I entered this weekend in terrific spirits because I'd just finished crushing the college football bowl games. I was 14–3, including a couple of all-star games! My biggest bets were on Army over Illinois in the Peach Bowl and Michigan over Nebraska in the Fiesta Bowl.

Illinois was picked by a tout service as one of those stupid "lock" games, and the points on them went from an opening of 6 all the way to 10 in some places. That was ridiculous on its face, and even more so when game day dawned in a downpour of rain. I loaded up. Army's superior ground attack won the contest, 31–29.

I took Michigan minus-3 because I liked its quarterback better than Nebraska's, and because I thought Nebraska's lack of a passing game doomed it if it ever got behind. Also, Nebraska was used to overpowering teams offensively and didn't figure to be able to do that to a tough Michigan defense. Michigan won the game handily.

The pro playoffs didn't go badly for me, either. I was 3–1 for the weekend.

THE WINS:

Cleveland plus-11 at Miami   Never watch an important game with a pessimist. My friend Moe watched the Miami place kicker put the opening kickoff into the end zone in this one, and said, "We're dead." I preferred to reserve judgment. Before I knew it, the Browns' running game had given them a 21–3 lead.

I liked this game mainly because 11 points is a lot to get on an NFL playoff contest. Cleveland had a top-notch defense, and it stuffed the Dolphins early while the Browns' runners chewed out the yards and the touchdowns.

But like someone who'd come into sudden wealth, the Browns didn't know how to handle it. The hot Miami weather in January seemed to wear down the Browns' backs, and between possessions the TV cameras showed them, wet towels over their heads, gulping oxygen on the sidelines. Meantime, Miami quarterback Marino began finding his receivers. Miami pulled it out, 24–21. Too bad. I found myself rooting for the underdog Browns to advance.

Los Angeles Rams minus-1 at home versus Dallas   I made this game 3½ points in favor of the Rams. I got the 1 point at Caesars late in the week. I didn't love it; I hesitated to bet against the veteran Cowboys in an important contest. But the Rams had youth and strength on their side, an excellent offensive line, and a great running back in Eric Dickerson, while the Cowboys had been getting by on guile. Score another for youth and strength. The Rams buried them, 20–0.

New England plus-6 at the Los Angeles Raiders   The Patriots were on a hot streak—12 straight wins against the points—and I went with them for number 13. The 6 points made me very comfortable. I made the game

Raiders minus-3, and with the 6 I had three ways to win or tie if the game had gone into overtime (a field goal by either team or a touchdown by mine).

The Patriots had just beaten the Jets on the road and had an edge in balance over the Raiders, whose Marc Wilson was only getting by at quarterback. Also, the Raiders' wide receivers weren't what they used to be. I'm sure that Al Davis will devote his off-season to acquiring some better ones.

This turned out to be the best game of the weekend. The Raiders took the lead but the Patriots' defense forced some turnovers (again) and fought back. New England won, 27–20.

The game produced the best TV ad-lib of the season. NBC's Merlin Olsen isn't noted for his wit, but when four Patriot pass rushers poured in on Wilson he hollered, "It looks like a jailbreak!"

And if my main-bet win wasn't enough, I cashed another that fewer than 21 points would be scored in the second half.

THE LOSS:

New York Giants plus-10 at Chicago   Last impressions make a lasting impression. The Bears had last week off while the Giants were whomping San Francisco. It made me rate New York higher than I should have.

Whatever the Giants lacked showed up against the Bears. Chicago's defensive blitzes and stunts intimidated New York, and their offensive line made Lawrence Taylor, the Giants' great linebacker, disappear. It was a close game for a half, mostly because Bears' kicker Keith Butler missed a couple of field-goal attempts in a stiff Soldier Field wind. But the Giants absolutely couldn't move on offense for the first three quarters, and it was too late by the fourth. I thought that 10 points would hold up in the Windy City chill, and I paid 6 to 5 to get my last half-point. I was wrong. Bears 21, Giants, 0.

WEEK 3

Oops! I blew my winning playoff edge this week by going down the tubes on both conference-title games. I haven't done that in quite a while. I guess I had it coming after my bowl-game feast and 3–1 NFL mark last week.

THE LOSSES:

Los Angeles Rams plus-11 at Chicago   Why did I favor the Rams over the rough-and-tough Bears? I don't know. Why do guys fall in love with ugly women?

This was mainly a bet on the weather and the points. Sure, the Bears were good, but 11 points is a lot in a conference-championship game with cold weather forecast. And with Dickerson running behind his big offensive line, it seemed to me like the Rams could control the ball long enough to at least hold down the score. I'd make the same bet again under the same circumstances.

But Old Man Winter took the day off in Chicago (the temperature was in the balmy high 30s), and so did Dieter Brock, the Rams' quarterback. All afternoon, his passes looked lonely bouncing around on my otherwise empty TV screen. I think the Bears' pass rush scared him the way it did the Giants' Phil Simms the week before. A small proposition-bet win that Dickerson would outrush the Bears' Walter Payton didn't make up for my main-bet loss. Chicago 24, Rams zilch.

Miami plus-4 at home versus New England   I made a small wager on the Dolphins here. Their great home-field record (one loss in the last two seasons, straight up) and my guess that the Pats were due for a fall after two road playoff wins were the convincers. I also liked the fact that Miami coach Don Shula had been in many, many big playoff games, while this was the first go-around for new coach Ray Berry of the Patriots.

Miami went out and played one of its worst games in a long time. It gave up four fumbles and two pass interceptions. New England ran the ball against the weak Miami rushing defense, and then ran it some more. New England 31, Miami 14.

SUPER BOWL SUNDAY

Sorry, faithful readers, but my 13-year Super Bowl winning streak was snapped by the mighty (almighty?) Bears. It had to happen the year I'm writing a book! There's no justice.

I knew that the Bears had a great defense in their "46," but I figured that, with two weeks to prepare a game plan, the Patriots would come up with some tricks to pierce it. I thought they'd go to a shotgun attack or use a lot of roll-outs to take advantage of the Bears' blitzing. Their quarterback, Tony Eason, is young and agile, and he could handle it. And, of course (you should know my thinking by now), 11 points on the *Super Bowl* game was more than I could pass up. I fully expected the Bears to win this one. It was the final score—46–10—that was the shocker.

The Bears, I think, caught the whole league off guard this season. Their defense was about the best and most ferocious I've ever seen. All 11 players on the unit seemed to do the right thing on every play all through the playoffs. They had supreme confidence in each other and in their defensive coach, Buddy Ryan. I think that if the Pats had come out with machine guns and opened fire on the Bears' defenders, the bullets would have bounced off the Bears' chests. That's how high they were.

Meantime, the Bears' attack was nicely balanced. Jim McMahon, their wise-guy quarterback, gave them a decent passing game for the first time since the days of Sid Luckman. The Bears are a young team and, unless injuries or dissension or fat-headedness set in, they should be contenders for the next four or five years. I bet the "over" at 36 points on this game, but I still wound up on the minus side for the day.

It was a bad way to end the NFL season, but, again, I can't complain. My winning percentage of almost 58 percent during the regular schedule was a bit under average for me, but it wasn't bad after my 0–6 first week and it put me solidly in the black on the NFL for the year.

As a gambler, I know better than to expect to win 13 straight at anything, but I must admit I liked the feeling, and I'll try to start a new streak on Super Bowl XXI in 1987. So while the football fans of Chicago are celebrating, I'll give you an old Chicago Cubs' baseball line: Wait till next year!